Chapters of Spirituality

WORLD YOGA CONVENTION 2013
GANGA DARSHAN, MUNGER, BIHAR, INDIA
23rd–27th October 2013

Chapters of Spirituality

Swami Niranjanananda Saraswati

Discourses from the Yogadristhi (Yogavision) series of satsangs at Baidyanatheshwar Shankarbag (Shivalaya), Munger, from 5th to 8th March, 2013

Yoga Publications Trust, Munger, Bihar, India

Published by Yoga Publications Trust
First edition 2013

ISBN: 978-93-81620-95-3

Publisher and distributor: Yoga Publications Trust, Ganga Darshan, Munger, Bihar, India.

Website: www.biharyoga.net
www.rikhiapeeth.net

Printed at Aegean Offset Printers, Greater Noida

Dedication

To our guru Sri Swami Satyananda Saraswati
who continues to inspire and guide us
on our spiritual journey.

Contents

What is Spirituality?

Morning, 5 March 2013

This year, on the occasion of Magha Poornima, I travelled on a pilgrimage to the Kumbha Mela at Prayag. The Kumbha is one of the largest spiritual congregations in the world. The Poorna Kumbha or the 'full' Kumbha is held every twelve years and the scriptures say that during this time, the gods, goddesses, siddhas and great souls from all realms visit the mela in their subtle body. The place no longer remains just the Kumbha City, but becomes the city of gods, of liberation and grace.

Among those who travelled with me to the Kumbha, was Swami Suryaprakash. This was his first visit to such a place where so many sadhus, sages and devotees were gathered in such large numbers. Watching them and observing what each of them were doing in their own camp, the teachings they were propagating, the sadhanas they were practising, and the religious beliefs they were espousing, he asked me a question, "Swamiji, what really is spirituality? Who is a spiritual person? There is a crowd of thirty million people here. Everyone has come to take a bath at the Kumbha Mela. Some are poor people from villages whose only luggage is a bundle on their head and they are here with their entire family. There are rich people who have access to all amenities. What faith has inspired these two poles of society to meet here? Eminent sadhus and mahamandaleshwaras are giving satsangs and lectures. Why have they come here? What is spirituality to them? A naga baba who has renounced everything is also sitting here, naked, smoking a chillum. What sadhana does he do and how does he go through life? What is spirituality to him?"

When Swami Suryaprakash posed such questions, I decided to answer them in this series of satsangs. Therefore, the subject of this satsang series is discovering what spirituality is and how it can be lived, the methods or mindsets that need to be employed, the traits that need to be developed, the virtues and qualities that need to be cultivated; how spiritual life can be lived and how one can become a better human being.

A lot has been spoken about spirituality, and people say one must become spiritual, yet have you ever thought about what real spirituality is? Is it just renouncing the world, the comforts and the luxuries of life? Is it leaving behind attachments and associations? Is it renunciation? Is it knowledge? Is it cultivation of the positive? Is it religion? Is it meditation? Is it yoga? What is spirituality?

Spirituality is a small word, yet so much mystery and meaning is hidden in it; it includes so many practices, mentalities, feelings, behaviours and conducts. If one contemplates the idea, one will understand its importance and usefulness.

Two groups of spiritual seekers

There are two kinds of people in the world: householders and ascetics. Both groups were gathered at the Kumbha Mela. The first group is engaged and involved in society, family, professional life, obligations and commitments. They are the regular people in society with ambitions and aspirations. The other group includes the renunciates, tyagis, sannyasins, naga babas, acharyas and mahamandaleshwaras of different ashrams and centres.

What does spirituality mean to these two groups? There is a clear distinction between the concept of spirituality perceived by the ascetics and the householders, which helps

to shed light on the understanding of spirituality. These two different groups follow different paths and ideas; they do not follow the same path, ideas or sadhana, although they may follow the same philosophy. They may follow the same school of thought; however, their sadhana, lifestyle, approach and expectations are totally different.

Spirituality for the householder

In spiritual life, the householders are searching for an intervention in their life in order to experience physical, psychological and spiritual wellbeing; a kind of divine, godly or saintly intervention to overcome their problems, difficulties and trials in life. This group of spiritual seekers is looking to spiritual life to find relief from their troubles and become happy, contented, satisfied and creative. This is their main purpose for cultivating spiritual life.

Not everyone who goes to the Kumbha Mela is seeking emancipation or moksha. Many are propelled only by the strength of their faith, conviction and belief that 'By undertaking this pilgrimage I will attain my desire. I will receive the grace to overcome my difficulties, poverty and sufferings in life. Maybe I will discover someone who can become the medium for divine intervention in my life, to improve the quality of my life so I can become more pious, loving, kind and compassionate.' For regular social people, this is the understanding of spiritual life.

The path of spirituality for householders leads them to become good in action, thought and behaviour. It makes them happier, less attached, more generous and compassionate, less selfish and more fulfilled. Their concept of spirituality is to develop a sattwic nature. It is enough for them to have the *shraddha*, faith, that 'By visiting the Kumbha all our sins will be washed away. By taking a bath in the Sangam we will receive the grace of God and the blessings of saints. Our unhappiness, lack, pain and poverty will all disappear.' Inspired by this sentiment, householders take part in the Kumbha Mela by the millions. The poorest of the poor and the oldest of the old walk with faltering feet, carrying bundles on their heads and shivering in the cold.

What is the force that is attracting them to the confluence, to the mela? The force is faith. There is no power stronger than faith. If a person has faith, the greatest mountain can be crossed; if there is no faith, one will accept defeat after walking ten steps.

Spirituality for sannyasins

The other group of spiritual seekers includes the renunciates, the sadhus and sannyasins. They understand spiritual life as an integral part of material life. Spiritual experiences are perceived as natural events in the course of their material life. They seek to improve the quality of their mind and emotions, and experience their inner nature. This is the concept of spirituality from the perspective of the renunciates.

At the Kumbha Mela, there were ascetics, sannyasins, mahamandaleshwaras and babas, some of whom lived simply and some who had every comfort at their disposal. They were repositories of knowledge and wisdom, as well as adepts at sadhana and austerities. Why do all these different types of sannyasins and sadhus gather at the Kumbha Mela? Is it to meet with each other, to purify themselves, or to receive divine grace? The concept of spirituality for the renunciates is discovery of the self.

After seeing and spending some time with the naga sadhus, I felt that these people have not wasted their time. Instead, they have gone beyond a certain state of mind or level of consciousness. Through their efforts in sadhana and intense austerities, they have fixed their mind on their *ishta*, chosen form of God, and guru. The deeper the focus on the ishta and guru, the greater is the purification and transformation. Through their mental purity and the effects of their austerities, they have attained inner knowledge. Undoubtedly, there are those who do not follow the path in an appropriate manner and pursue desires, yet some are sincerely devoted to spiritual life. The true aspirants have been able to still the dissipations and desires of the mind, and awakened their inner light and radiance.

There were acharyas, mandaleshwaras and mahamandaleshwaras who lived like kings, yet were infinite storehouses of knowledge, like walking knowledge banks. When they spoke, they would quote from the Puranas, the *Rig Veda*, the *Atharva Veda*, the Upanishads and the smritis. Through their attainments, new understandings, thinking and behaviour have developed. What they do with their attainment is up to them; they may choose to keep the knowledge to themselves or disseminate it. Nevertheless, on the strength of *jnana*, wisdom, they have been able to develop new perspectives on life and acquire an understanding of the path of virtue and dharma. Not only do they try to follow this path themselves, they also inspire others to do so.

Power of faith

Householders, both poor and rich, come to the Kumbha Mela with some desire or wish, and the motor that drives that desire is shraddha, faith. If the motor of faith does not exist, then one will not be able to focus on the wish or desire. If you want to see living faith, if you want to see faith and devotion walking and moving in action, there is no better place than the Kumbha.

After all, thirty million people go there with pure faith, devotion and feeling. This is not baseless. Their devotion and faith is the energy that takes them across the sea of suffering and establishes them in the kingdom of grace and peace. This is the meaning and foundation of the subject of spirituality. Whether a householder or an ascetic, in essence all have come to attain the compassion and grace of God, from which they receive inner strength, love, the power of endurance to face the struggles of life, and the learning to always keep smiling.

What is the Truth?

Afternoon, 5 March 2013

In ancient times there lived a rishi couple named Atri and Anasuya. Both were great ascetics, renunciates and siddhas; however, they had no children. In the tradition of rishis, those who lead a spiritual life also have to fulfil the duties of a householder and produce progeny. One day, the thought of his childless state passed through Maharishi Atri's mind. On that very same day, he had an experience in meditation. He saw Brahma, Vishnu and Mahesh before him and all the three gods lifted their hands. The light coming out of their hands entered Maharishi Atri's body and he felt that he had received their blessings.

The same night Anasuya had a dream. It was not just a dream; it was a living experience. In the dream, she saw the three gods knocking at her door. Mother Anasuya opened the door and the three gods said, "*Bhiksham dehi!*" – "Give alms." There are three different types of food which can be offered to a mendicant asking for alms. If you offer food you have already made, it is considered ordinary food, *bhojana*. If the guest is asked what they would like to eat and that food is then prepared and offered, this is *iccha bhojana*, desired food. Food prepared at home and first offered to God or the divine is the third type of food, *prasad bhojana*. Such food is eaten as prasad and is distributed to both family and guests.

When Mother Anasuya asked the gods what they would like, they said, "We want iccha bhoj." She asked, "What kind of iccha bhoj would you like?" They said, "Feed us in the form of a mother, and we will take the form of children." Mother Anasuya shut her eyes and thought, 'These gods are testing my purity, sanctity and the strength of my sadhana. They have expressed a wish that I should look upon them as children and myself in the form of a mother. I shall fulfil their wish.' She saw all the three gods becoming children, and she placed them on her lap and breastfed them. In this manner, they were given iccha bhoj. At this point, the dream ended. When she woke up she knew that the gods had blessed her with children.

What is the truth?

After some time, Atri and Anasuya became parents to three divine, extraordinary children. The first child was known as Chandrama, believed to be an incarnation of Brahma, the creator. The second was Rishi Durvasa, an incarnation of Shiva. The third was Dattatreya, an incarnation of Vishnu. The three were spiritually inclined right from birth and became saints of repute in their time.

Chandrama and Durvasa left home during childhood to perform austerities and find their own path and destiny. Dattatreya stayed home with Atri and Anasuya until the age of eighteen, participating in the routine of the ashram. At the age of eighteen, he went to his parents and with folded hands, asked for permission to leave so he too could follow the path of sadhana.

Naturally, Anasuya was not pleased about her only remaining son leaving home, but she was also a rishi, a learned woman, the person who gave birth to divine children. She said, "I will give you permission only if you answer a question of mine." Dattatreya asked, "What is your question, mother?" Anasuya said, "Son, what is the truth?"

Dattatreya said, "The search for truth is the most important goal and aim of human life. What you consider to be the truth is not truth at all. The truth is that which no one has been able to perceive until today. Shiva is truth. Shiva is

Satyam-Shivam-Sundaram – Truth-Auspiciousness-Beauty. That which is true, auspicious and beautiful is the highest power. It is distant from us. We are not able to know it. However, the one who is able to know the truth, to know auspiciousness and to know beauty, is able to understand the Supreme Element pervading the creation. Such a one becomes united with the Supreme Element and attains liberation from samsara.

"In this creation we are performing our respective roles on account of the Supreme Element. Within all of us, we have the same Supreme Element which is the truth, eternal and unchangeable. It is auspicious, giving the experience of happiness and contentment. It is beauty, containing peace, contentment and fullness.

"We are not able to experience this Supreme Element in this body, as the body, matter and maya bind us. It is on account of maya that we believe the world to be the truth and are not able to know that Supreme Element. The two are so intertwined with each other that it becomes impossible to separate them. It is only when you withdraw your attention from worldly matters and connect with the Supreme Spirit, *Paramatma*, that you will discover the difference between truth and untruth, reality and illusion.

"This world is not the Supreme Element, for its nature is change. It is a transient phenomenon. Therefore, never believe the world and its experiences to be the truth. Try to know and understand what is beyond it, as only that is the truth, that is Shiva, that is beauty, and that is the Supreme Element." He continued, "Mother, just as there are twelve hours in the day and the night, and during daytime you see the whole creation and at night you see only darkness, in the same manner this life is also divided into two compartments. One compartment is the material and physical which you identify with, and the other is the spiritual. You have to discover what your spiritual life is. The material life is conditioned and tainted by the quality of tamas, and the inner, spiritual life is coloured by the quality of sattwa. When you are born in this material life, the tamasic conditioning takes over. Therefore, an additional effort has to be made to realize that tamasic, destructive, negative conditioning and to transform it into a creative, positive force. That is the journey of a spiritual aspirant, the movement from tamas to sattwa.

"Once you have attained the sattwa nature, the sattwa quality, then you realize the eternal truth, auspiciousness and beauty. The combination of truth, auspiciousness and beauty make the body of God.

"Truth is God as it never changes. This world is not the truth, as here everything keeps changing every moment, every hour, every day. Thus, despite appearances, this material world is unreal and impermanent, whereas the spiritual world is real, the permanent state of the Supreme

Spirit. In the span of infinity, you take birth and live this life for eighty to ninety years, and for those years of your stay in the world, you think it to be real, and your permanent place to be unreal. Yet, how is that possible? This is the unreal place, for once you leave here, after your term is over, where will you go back to? To your original home. Therefore, mother, know that this world is impermanent, unreal and tamasic, and the higher world is composed of truth, auspiciousness and beauty. There is nothing detrimental or negative there; everything is good, auspicious, uplifting, constructive and creative. When you are able to perceive life and yourself as part of Satyam-Shivam-Sundaram, mother, know that you have realized the divinity within you."

Sadhana of remembrance

Mother Anasuya then asked Dattatreya, "How do I cultivate awareness of this higher reality?" Dattatreya gives a beautiful answer. He says, "Mother, there is only one sadhana for you, and that is the sadhana of remembrance, of one-pointedness of mind leading to concentration, the sadhana of *ekagrata*. Beyond that you do not need anything more." Dattatreya said to his mother, "Make your mind centred on your *aradhya*, the one you worship, and then don't move it from there. Keep it fixed there."

This sadhana is easy for all mothers, as when a child goes away and the mother is left alone at home, she remembers her child constantly. Even while she is engaged in work, whether it is cleaning, sweeping, washing or cooking, she keeps the memory of her child alive in her mind. One aspect of her mind is linked with her child, continuously remembering, thinking about and visualizing the child. That is the sadhana of remembrance and concentration. In the same way, as a mother remembers her child, when a devotee always remembers his aradhya, his dissipated mind becomes quiet and concentrated.

Dattatreya told his mother only one thing, "All you have to do is keep your mind fixed on your aradhya. Keep doing

all your work. There is no need to change anything, just change your perspective."

Mother Anusuya said, "How will I remember my aradhya when I am so attached to you?" Dattatreya replied, "Keep doing all your work; there is no need to change anything, just change your perspective. Mother, do not change your nature. If you are attached, remain attached, but not to the world; attach yourself to the higher reality. Simply detach yourself from the world and attach yourself to the higher reality. If you desire something, are passionate about something, or infatuated by something, let those conditions and states remain. The only thing that you need to do is connect these expressions and sentiments to a positive aspect, rather than the negative, materialistic aspect. If you want to remain attached, attach yourself to God. If you want to remain passionate, fine; however, not in the world, express your passion in spiritual life. In this way, divert your mind from the material to the spiritual identity, and identify with the purity of truth, auspiciousness and beauty. Remove the worldly feeling and establish the feeling for God. This is all you have to do. If you are able to do this, you will experience Satyam-Shivam-Sundaram." Saying this, Dattatreya left the ashram.

Completeness of human life

The teaching that Dattatreya gave to his mother became the foundation for the discovery of the spiritual nature in individuals. Rishi Dattatreya propagated the concept that God is truth, auspiciousness and beauty, and attaining Him is spirituality. However, when the spirit comes into this world, the mind, emotions and body assume a tamasic covering, therefore one is unable to see the path of life clearly. One can only see the obstacles. Your first duty is to remove these obstacles through the process of sadhana.

Where do these obstacles come from? To know this, it is necessary to understand some facts about creation and life. This creation of God is indescribable and endless. It is said that the whole creation consists of 8.4 million types of living beings. Amongst these, only one creature has a mind and that is the human being. Every creature has a purpose and a dharma. Human life also has an aim, a purpose, a duty and a dharma. What is this dharma? To gain victory over matter, mind and emotions.

People often think of spirituality as self-realization or God-realization, yet if you look at the teachings of the saints, sages and sannyasins of both past and present, what are they trying to teach? Everybody chooses one method which becomes their rubberstamp. The Buddha chose meditative techniques such as vipassana and anapanasatti to lead one to the point of nothingness, *nirvana*. These are practices of pratyahara. Maharshi Mahesh Yogi chose one meditative technique commonly known as Transcendental Meditation, and that is a practice of ajapa japa, one of the practices of dharana.

In this manner, each teacher has picked up one item of thought and practice according to the need of the society at the given time, and has propagated that. Sri Swami Satyananda Saraswati developed and offered yoga nidra as the solution to overcome the tensions and stresses of the human psyche and life. However, does that make him the preacher, teacher or propagator of only that particular practice? No. Similarly, it would be wrong to say that that the teachings of Buddha are confined to vipassana, anapanasatti and other techniques. The realized people have used these as tools to turn on the switch of spiritual life within.

Human life has been given a purpose, reason, direction and aim. The human life is known as *manushi* or rational life; the thinking, rational, intellectual life form. It has three main functions: to attain mastery over matter, attain mastery over mind and attain mastery over emotions. These are the three defined areas for a human being to live and to excel in. Once mastery has been attained over these three aspects, then one progresses to the next stage of evolution, into the next life form.

From one perspective, spiritual life begins when you start to become aware of your dharma and karma in life. The dharma of human life is transcendence of the body, mind and emotions. The karma, then, is any method that can be adopted to achieve this. The starting point towards this is extending one's awareness to develop the knowledge and understanding of how the body, mind and emotions work, influence and alter your nature, personality and responses.

When you were born, you were given this body and you slowly learnt how to use it. At first, you did not even know how to walk, eat or speak; however, as you grew older, you began to know your body, use it and control it. The same was true of the mind. When you were born, you did not know how to use the mind, you did not know about the intellect or the emotions. As you grew older, you educated and improved yourself, you involved yourself in work and duty, and started understanding the mind, its strengths and weaknesses, its patterns, and how to use it. The same is the case with emotions. Thus, to develop mastery and be victorious over matter, mind and emotional energy is what brings fullness to human life.

Bhoga and yoga

The soul entering the body is pure, yet the body is not pure. Since the soul is energy, it is strength. The mind is also energy. However, the body is matter, made up of five elements. In the process of coming into being, the individual spirit goes through transformation from the purity of spirit to the impurity of matter. The soul and the mind, both in the form of energy, become locked inside the material body. Therefore, the qualities or the nature the manifested being expresses is that of the body, tainted by the colours of maya.

The nature of the body is material, sensorial and tamasic. Matter connects with *bhoga*, enjoyment, while energy connects with *yoga*, union and harmony. That is why the body desires enjoyment. The body wants everything to be pleasurable and comfortable; it never wants to have any difficulty or pain. The mind, however, does not want enjoyment, as enjoyment makes the mind distracted. The mind wants peace. The body wants enjoyment and comfort, while the mind wants peace. You must have experienced this in your life. In spite of having all kinds of comfort, luxuries, enjoyment and wealth, the mind is not at peace, as wealth, property and prosperity do not give peace. Rather, there is a greater feeling of restlessness.

The body's nature, which is attracted to enjoyment, sensorial pleasure and comfort, is *tamoguni*, the quality of inertia, ignorance, darkness, negativity. When you are attracted towards the sense objects of enjoyment, it is an expression of tamoguna and when you make the effort to attain peace, it is an expression of *sattwa guna*, luminosity, peace, balance and purity. When you are attracted to enjoyment, the mind and behaviour are controlled by the senses and sense objects. When the mind and body aspire for peace, you are separated from the sense objects. In the same manner that a tortoise withdraws its body parts into its shell, you gather yourself into your inner being and experience peace when the mind and senses are withdrawn from the sense objects.

Therefore, bhoga and yoga are two opposite poles in life. Enjoyment is an expression of tamoguna, whereas yoga is an expression of sattwa guna. The journey that takes you from tamoguna towards sattwa guna is known as spirituality, and it involves the process of sadhana.

Obstacles in spiritual life

Paramguru Swami Sivananda says that when one is born into this tamasic nature and condition of life and the world, one has to face many obstacles in the endeavour towards liberation and cultivating the positive, uplifting qualities in life. If awareness of these obstacles is heightened and one makes an effort to avoid or manage them, then happiness and peace are attainable.

The first obstacle is the state of duality, the feeling of 'I' and 'you'; the separation between oneself and others, the divisions of high and low, rich and poor, haves and have-nots, good and bad. This is duality and it splits the mind and the personality, so there is no unity in one's nature, thought or expression. There is a split between one's personal philosophy and one's actions; one's aspirations and ideas do not match one's actions.

Duality does not allow you to accept your circumstances in life, and you begin to feel anger, malice and hatred. In the twelfth chapter of the *Bhagavad Gita*, the first quality of a bhakta that Sri Krishna mentions is freedom from malice

towards all. Do not foster malice, envy or hatred towards anyone. If you are malicious towards another, you have not risen above duality.

Diversity is also an obstacle. Whenever you see variety, the mind is attracted to it. It flitters like a honeybee from flower to flower. This tendency becomes the cause of mental and emotional dissipation. The mind is never still, concentrated and peaceful. In the olden days, people would say, "Oh, I don't like this clothing, let me buy a new set." Then it became, "I don't like this bicycle, let me buy a motorcycle." Then it became, "I don't like this Ambassador car, let me buy a BMW." Nowadays it has become, "I don't like my husband; I want to change my husband", "I don't like my wife; I want to change my wife." Everything has become a commodity and you think that relationships and associations can be changed just as you change clothes, food, television and car. This is the outcome of mental dissipation, where the mind is not focused and is pulled in different directions by different sense objects. In such a state, you cannot find peace anywhere. You become totally hypnotized by and focused on the material dimension: achievements, comforts, luxuries. As a result, you become a self-oriented, selfish being. That is the tamasic conditioning.

Other obstacles include the feeling of worthlessness, arrogance, vanity, pride, attraction, repulsion, fear of the unknown, sensuality, oversensitivity, emotionality, idleness, weakness and sickness. They are all the influences of the negative, tamasic nature and conditioning in your life. Swami Sivananda lists these obstacles in the form of a song called *Obstacles to God-Realization*:

Duality, Multiplicity, Plurality,
Individuality, Slave Mentality, Dadabadality,
Gadabadality, Dambhacharity, Asmitaity,
Ahamkarity, Raga-Dveshity, Abhiniveshity,
Sensuality, Sensitivity, Sentimentality,
Inactivity, Rotundity,
Are the obstacles to attain Divinity,
Universality, Cosmicality, Real Unity.
Debility, Morbidity, Anemiaty,
Pyorrheaty, Blood-Pressurity,
Myopiaty, Presbyopiaty, Amblyopiaty
Nyctalopiaty, Hemianopiaty, Doctor's Mahafoolishnessity,
Maha-Andhakaraity,
Are the obstacles to attain Divinity.
Atrocity, Curiosity, Cruelty,
Anxiety, Partiality, Timidity,
Duality, Individuality, Immorality,
Debility, Morbidity, Sensuality,
These are the obstacles to attain Divinity.

If you can overcome this tamasic conditioning, and cultivate instead the sattwic qualities, then your life will become a divine life. That divinity is truth-auspiciousness-beauty. This idea of spirituality was given by Sage Dattatreya in a concise form and has been further developed by other traditions and luminaries of human civilization.

Approaches to Spirituality

Morning, 6 March 2013

Two groups can be found in society: one is that of householders, engaged in society and the world; and the other is that of ascetics, trying to disengage from the normal social patterns and instead focus on experiencing, attaining and expressing something qualitatively different in life. One group has material aspirations and the other group has spiritual aspirations. Those engaged in society have material aspirations and those who are trying to disengage themselves take to the path of renunciation to experience, explore, understand, realize and express a different way of life. How is spirituality realized by these two groups of people?

Two approaches to spirituality

Spirituality for both groups means something different. The regular worldly individual in society only wants freedom from suffering, not liberation; they are looking for peace, happiness, contentment and quietude. They want to live a life free from distractions, disturbances and tensions; one in which they are comfortable, happy, content and able to express whatever they wish to express in life. To ask a householder, "Do you want liberation?" is foolish, as that is not his aim. The aim of a householder is to live in comfort, luxury and peace without tension or difficulty. If possible, he may like to do something to uplift society. This is the basic mentality in a worldly person's life. How will spirituality be realized in such an individual's life?

On the other hand, there is another group that says, "I have to discover the spiritual nature, which is the discovery of *Satyam-Shivam-Sundaram,* truth-auspiciousness-beauty in life." Spirituality, therefore, is not a discipline, dogma, or a belief system; it is a spontaneous appreciation, worship and adoration of life. Religions are dogmas, belief systems, traditions and ideas, which can be followed from time to time. Spirituality, however, is a process of attaining personal transformation, purity and upliftment. Spirituality is qualitatively changing the expressions and behaviours of life, and the discovery of truth-auspiciousness-beauty.

The ascetic makes an attempt to attain freedom from worldly attachment and separates himself from society. While the worldly individual is engrossed in the world and sense objects, a person free from worldly attachment adopts a disinterested attitude towards the world and material life. A worldly person is steeped in infatuation, an individual free from worldly attachment creates a disconnection from infatuation; a worldly person remains fascinated by desires, an ascetic keeps away from desires. The ordinary mentality adopted by a worldly person is changed by a sadhu, an ascetic and an individual who is free from involvement in the world of sense objects.

Sage Dattatreya described God as the form of truth-auspiciousness-beauty. To attain this is every individual's quest, whether it be a householder or a sannyasin. The householder tries to find spirituality in *bhoga* or enjoyment, and the sannyasin in yoga; there is a difference between the two. The meaning of spirituality is to connect with the purity of the spirit and to live in purity. This purity touches every sphere of life, whether material, social, familial, professional or spiritual.

Six enemies of spiritual life

When one is born into this life, one comes with a particular type of mindset: a dualistic mentality. This becomes the cause of problems in life, as it gives birth to the awareness of 'you' and 'I' as separate entities. It gives the idea of high and low, better and worse, good and bad, right and wrong, positive and negative. The more these concepts of duality are allowed to grow, the more impressions and dissipations are created in the mind. The cause of suffering in life is duality, and it has six offspring: *kama* or passion; *krodha* or aggression; *lobha or* greed; *moha* or infatuation; *mada* or arrogance; and *matsarya* or jealousy. These are the children of duality. They are the six enemies one has to confront on the spiritual journey, as they control and govern one's life.

Spiritual practice for a householder

To cultivate spirituality, a householder uses various methods such as fasts, worship, mantra japa, pilgrimages, staying in the company of sadhus and saints, and so on. They follow spirituality as a means to attain the divine grace that will ease their material life. That is known as *sakama aradhana*, self-oriented worship, invocation, or spirituality. This normal group of people has a common mentality: live a happy, tension-free life, with contentment, comfort and fulfilment, and be successful in every undertaking. When they find difficulties or barriers in the attainment of their desires, they go to temples and other places of worship to pray for the eradication of their difficulties and suffering, with the thought that 'If this pain and suffering go away, I'll once again become happy, content and fulfilled.'

As part of their sadhana, some people fast on the day of Ekadashi, and some on the full moon day. Some people have only fruit and some drink only water. There are various methods. The fast can be for one day or forty days, depending on the sankalpa and faith. Fasting purifies the body, mind and emotions. When the restlessness of the mind is calmed by fasting, worship becomes easy. That is why fasting is a practice recommended for householders. Various aspects of fasting can be looked into, such as what day to fast on and what should be eaten or avoided, in order to help facilitate other sadhanas. The aim is to maximize the positive effect on the body, prana, brain, mind and emotions, and to become balanced and fit. Thereafter, it becomes easy to perform whatever sadhana one undertakes.

Another method that the householder cultivates in spiritual life is to worship the family god or goddess; this constitutes the tradition of performing *pooja*. Those who have a guru perform the pooja with the guru mantra. Those who do not have a guru or a family god, only faith, can just light a lamp and incense. Whether the worship is performed for one second or done for hours with the chanting of mantras, for that time the mind is disconnected from material involvement and connected with divine energy. For that duration, peace, happiness and satisfaction are experienced. From the simple act of lighting incense and a lamp with the feeling, 'I am lighting incense and lamp before God', peace and contentment are experienced. The thought in the mind is, 'I will benefit from what I'm doing, as it is auspicious.' When this positive thought arises in the mind, the negative tendencies automatically disappear.

As part of spiritual life, householders also go on pilgrimages and visit places of worship. They pray for peace in the family or professional growth. In the *grihastha ashrama*, householder life, every person worships their chosen form of god inspired by one idea: 'Something good and auspicious will result from my worship, unhappiness will go away and I will attain happiness and success.' When life becomes favourable, they say, "I have the grace of God with me, everything is favourable."

Out of this group, some people decide to perform more difficult sadhanas, poojas, anushthanas and aradhanas so their difficulties may be resolved more quickly. Those who are disturbed by tension and worry, think that they will attain mental peace by doing some extra japa and meditation. In order to eradicate mental tensions, worries, disturbances and weaknesses, and to gain spiritual strength and willpower, they practise meditation.

Therefore, this group in society connects with spirituality to seek divine intervention for fulfilment of their needs. Once that intervention has taken place, they are happy and they do not seek anything more. This is the relationship that a householder, a worldly individual, establishes with God. Although this relationship is forged with an ulterior motive, it is also called *bhakti* or devotion, as God is still being worshipped. Thus, this path is also said to be worthwhile. Worship with a view to future gain has been given the form of bhakti for householders, as it connects them with the transcendental, uplifting force of the Supreme Spirit.

Spiritual sadhana of an ascetic

The ascetic also seeks truth-auspiciousness-beauty, but rather than searching for it in worldly enjoyment, he seeks it in yoga and renunciation. On the path of yoga, the first thing that happens is that the mind and the six enemies are confronted, and gradually the state of the mind changes. If you want to get to know your mind, then come and stay in the ashram for a month. If you are given only khichari to eat for six days in a row, your mind will rebel and say, 'I've eaten too much khichari, now I feel like having something tasty, tangy and spicy.' During such experiences you will discover how much strength and sway the mind has, and how it makes you reject the khichari and crave something tastier to eat. If a small thing like taste can disturb your mental balance and give birth to new desires and cravings, then imagine the havoc caused by the other senses in your life!

The students who spend a month in the ashram are asked if they are happy when they are about to leave. They answer, "Yes, Swamiji, we are very happy." Then we ask, "What will you do when you go home?" They say, "We will eat lots of food!" We ask, "Were you dying of hunger here?" They reply, "No Swamiji, we were not dying of hunger, but the food here is very plain and sattwic, and we want tasty, rajasic food." This is the condition of people's minds!

The process of renunciation in the life of a sadhu starts with the ability to confront the mind. All attachments, infatuations and desires must be given up. People think of renunciation as leaving one's house or society. That is not renunciation. There was a time when this was necessary; however, if renunciation were to be redefined, it relates to giving up attachment and attraction. The attraction and attachment to wife and husband, wealth and enjoyment must be renounced, not the wife and husband, wealth or enjoyment in themselves. Making an attempt to free oneself from the cause of bondage is non-attachment, and this is the effort of a sannyasin.

Renunciation does not mean renouncing home, family, friends and associations, unless they are the cause of your kama, krodha, mada or moha. If they are, then renounce them also. If they are not the cause of your passion, aggression and infatuation, then accept them. The human mind is weak, and one of its main habits is to latch on to something for its security, safety, fulfilment and happiness. You latch on to anything you lay your hands on, thinking, 'With this association I will become a bit happier than earlier,' without realizing that this craving to be happy leads to attachment and infatuation.

In the yogic and spiritual tradition, renunciation is related to giving up *tamas* or darkness, inertia and negativity. Transforming the tamasic mental state into a sattwic one is true renunciation. The scriptures, sages and seers say this is all you need to do to attain purity and experience God. The purpose of all sadhana is to gradually reduce one's material attachments and redirect the awareness from the world to God. When you are world-oriented, you become bound, and when you are God-oriented, you are liberated. This has been the central spiritual thought of India, which has given strength and energy to the path of renunciation.

An ascetic's spiritual journey starts with the mind. First, the mind must be confronted. This is where yoga sadhana comes in, as stated in Sage Patanjali's *Yoga Sutras* (1:2): *Yogaschitta vritti nirodhah* – "To block the patterns of consciousness and the restless fluctuations is yoga." Once these *chitta vrittis*, the modifications and restless fluctuations of the mind, cease and the mind stops running from one subject to another, it may enter the state of meditation. Concentration develops and the mind becomes one with the highest consciousness. This is the path of ascetics and it is related to the mind, whereas the path of the householders is related to circumstances. This is how spirituality and religion are different.

Religion and spirituality

Religion is an order, a belief, a faith, something to be treated with respect and awe; it is something that acts as a force not just for an individual, but for a whole society. Religion indicates an external social order, and by making one aware of the highest power, inspires one to identify and merge with that. It is an external, material arrangement that obliges one to think of God from time to time, as part of one's life in society.

Spirituality, on the other hand, is a personal and spontaneous process of inner transformation. The purpose

and task of a householder is to bring about a change in the circumstances. That is why spirituality for the householder is always related to circumstances. If there is suffering, worship is performed to end the suffering; they go to sadhus and saints and ask for their grace and blessings. All this is aimed at making life favourable, so there is happiness, peace and fulfilment. This gives rise to the experience of auspiciousness and beauty all around, and the Supreme Element is experienced in the material world itself.

This vision, however, is a reflection. Just as you see the reflection of yourself in a mirror, similarly, the householders see the vision of the Supreme Spirit in the world. The ascetic, however, does not focus on the reflection in the world. He perceives his own self as part of that divinity and identifies with it, seeing the reflection within. This path of the ascetic begins with the mind.

Basis of spirituality

As long as you identify with duality, you remain a materialistic person. The spiritual traditions say that spirituality is the overcoming of duality in life and the experience of universality, the experience of unity in diversity. The foundation of your spiritual development is the dawning of the ability to experience unity in duality. Even in the *Bhagavad Gita*, the first prerequisite for a spiritual aspirant defined by Sri Krishna is not asana, pranayama, relaxation, meditation, japa or mantra. The first guideline in the *Bhagavad Gita* is to overcome duality and see oneness in everyone, see the unifying factor in everyone. This is the first condition to becoming spiritual, according to Sri Krishna. It is also the first condition spoken of in the ancient teachings of saints and in scriptures. Duality is the barrier between the individual and the divine. When seen from a philosophical perspective, it becomes difficult to eradicate duality; however, if it is approached from a practical perspective, it becomes possible to manage duality and attain unity.

In order to develop a unified, singular vision, what is the sutra that should be followed? Recall when Anasuya asks her son, Dattatreya, "Son, what is the truth?" Dattatreya replies, "Mother, the only permanent thing in this dimension is Satyam-Shivam-Sundaram; the truth that does not change, that is eternal and permanent." If something changes, it is not eternal or permanent, therefore it cannot be the truth. Auspiciousness is that in which there is the possibility of attaining happiness, contentment and fulfilment. Beauty is that appreciation of life where there is no sadness, distraction or disturbance; everything is seen as the manifestation of the higher power. The nature of God is Satyam-Shivam-Sundaram; however, it cannot be realized by the individual due to the *dvaita bhava*, the dualistic mind. In another sense, the dualistic mind is a gift from nature to this creation, as nothing in creation or nature can be understood without it. The problem is that it creates a distance between yourself and your inner source. You identify with the creation, the material world and sense objects.

In the scriptures, the state of duality is considered to be the biggest fault of the mind. Due to this state, you view circumstances and people as good or bad, pleasant or unpleasant. It makes you think in terms of high and low, rich and poor. Duality gives you the impression of 'having' or 'not having'. It is the cause of your perception of the lack or prosperity in your life, your strengths and weaknesses. It places the mind in a constant state of fluctuation, since the mind sees two and finds itself wanting in its given circumstances. The dualistic mind always changes its intentions, so one is never comfortable, no matter where one is. The grass always looks greener on the other side of the fence. One never finds balance.

If you want spirituality to grow in your life, first you must put an end to this state of duality. The end of duality and the awakening of non-duality and unity is the bedrock of spirituality. In this process, the sutra to be followed is: "See yourself in everyone." As stated in the scriptures, try to see God in everything.

A clear understanding of how to overcome the duality of mind is given by Sri Swamiji when he speaks of cultivating *atmabhava*, the ability to see yourself in other people. For example, your child is sick with a high fever. The doctor has given medicines and is treating the child. The child is being taken care of, yet you spend sleepless nights by your child. Why do you not go to bed and sleep properly? Why do you have to stay up, and why do you stay up only with your child? Why will you not stay up when somebody else's child is sick? You do not express that same care and concern at that time. Why? The answer is simple: in your child you see a reflection of yourself, whereas in another child, you do not see your reflection. If you are able to see yourself in other people, then that reduces the dualistic mentality and cultivates atmabhava, the awareness which makes you see yourself in every object, in every other form. Therefore, reach out to all beings. Only then will the vision of duality end in your life.

Method to awaken atmabhava

Currently, you experience atmabhava only in your intimate associations, such as with your child, husband, wife, and close family members. If, however, you make this connection with others as well, and believe others to be your own, your life will become pure and divine.

Sri Swamiji illustrated the way to make this connection by giving a practical method of experiencing and cultivating atmabhava. He says that when you go to the market to buy clothes for your two children, think instead that you have three children, two who are your own and one who is unknown to you. Buy three of everything: clothes, shoes and bags. Give two sets to your children, and give the remaining set to some stranger who does not have it but deserves it. By giving that third set to an unknown child in need, you will bring joy and happiness into that life. That joy and happiness is worth millions of blessings by God. Will it not make you happy to see that joy in someone's face who is not considered your own, knowing that you have contributed to that happiness? Yes, it will also make you happy. Do this according to your means; if you have the means to buy for four, then buy for four. If you have the means to buy for four hundred, then buy for four hundred. Two for your own, and 398 for your unknown children. If you have the means, buy for four thousand children, two for your own and 3,398 for the other children. In this way, the cultivation of atmabhava gradually reduces the dualistic mentality and generates universality.

This is not charity, selfless service or duty to society. Remember this well. When atmabhava develops, this becomes your own experience and expression. See your own children in the same way that you see the children of others. The way you work for your own children, work for other children in the same way. When this idea does not just remain a thought and instead turns into an actual experience in your life, then you will be able to establish yourself in unity and non-duality, not before that. When you remain in the dualistic mentality, you think of yourself as both the doer and the enjoyer. When you begin to experience non-duality, you no longer believe yourself to be the doer or enjoyer, but consider yourself as just a medium through which auspicious work is completed; you become the medium of divine grace.

Entering the kingdom of God

Spirituality is not an order or a discipline. Religion is an order, a discipline, a belief and a faith; however, spirituality is the worship of life and of the beauty inherent in life. It is the search for peace in life and experience of the Supreme Element. One who rises above the state of duality and attains the state of oneness takes the first step into spiritual life.

The world and nature are composed of tamoguna. When you come to this world of sense objects in bodily form, the influences of tamoguna control the body and mind. The state of duality is where the kingdom of *maya*, illusion, begins. Due to maya, the mind remains confused. The state of duality is maya's strength. If, however, you manage to attain the state of non-duality, you will get the visa to enter the kingdom of God, of Paramatma, the Supreme Spirit. Then you will be able to go there whenever you want; you can go on a pilgrimage, receive darshan and come back.

Reflections of sages

A sadhu has a particular way of thinking: 'Staying in this world is not the aim of my life. The aim of my life is to attain God. What should I do for that? How do I experience that Supreme Element? For that, I must free myself from the obstacles that bring destruction and downfall.' These obstacles are the six enemies in everyone's life: *kama*, lust; *krodha*, anger; *lobha*, greed; *moha*, infatuation; *mada*, arrogance; and *matsarya*, jealousy. These are the six children of duality, due to which strife, problems, difficulties, conflicts, confusions, and all types of psychological upheavals, mental problems and difficulties arise. The sadhu first struggles with and attempts to overcome these six enemies.

The dualistic mentality, with its six offspring, creates havoc in one's life. Thus, sannyasins begin their journey with

the idea of renunciation. They renounce those things that bind them, and adopt those that can help reduce the weight of the six enemies. The weight must reduce. Renunciation means to reduce the baggage. If you have fifty kilos of baggage and can carry only twenty, you will renounce thirty kilos. A sannyasin will try to renounce forty-nine kilos and carry only one kilo. Renouncing and reducing the weight is known as *chhorna*, leaving behind. The spiritual journey of a sannyasin begins with leaving behind the dualistic mind, passion, aggression, greed, infatuation, arrogance and envy.

The last chapter of the *Brihadaranyaka Upanishad* says that the fires of lust, anger and greed burn a *manushi*, the human being; they destroy human life and existence. One who can bear their heat is a sadhu, and one who cannot bear their heat contracts mental problems and diseases. If lust, anger, greed, infatuation, arrogance and jealousy are strong and their disturbances go on for months and years in the head, what will be the state? There will be no peace. The mind will become restless, dissipated, unbalanced, aggressive and gross. That is why spirituality for a sannyasin begins with renunciation and non-attachment.

As far as *shraddha*, faith, is concerned, it applies to both the householder and the sannyasin. However, if in householder life spirituality begins with faith and its growth brings happiness, in the lives of sadhus, faith is strengthened with renunciation. Renunciation is the basis for attaining freedom from the six enemies. Until this freedom is attained, there will be no peace, even in the Himalayas. Once this freedom is attained, you will not hear noise in the midst of a busy market, due to the peace and quiet within.

To develop spiritual power and inner strength, one has to realize and eradicate the negative influences of the destructive conditions and traits of mind. For that, 'leaving behind the extra baggage' must be the theme. The idea of *tyaga*, renunciation, is cultivating this spiritual awareness, which is the destiny of every human being. Without renunciation, one cannot cultivate spiritual awareness. One can experience the spiritual nature, the awakened nature, the untainted nature of consciousness only by renouncing and staying away from the influences and effects of the six enemies of life. Avoid those things that stain the purity, simplicity, innocence and strength of consciousness. The one who adopts the path of renunciation by confronting the six enemies and is able to become free from the tamasic influences, reaches the heights of spirituality. Such a one gradually becomes a sadhu, a saint, and develops a unique way of thinking with a different perspective on life and creation.

Cultivating a Divine Life

Afternoon, 6 March 2013

Human beings have organized themselves into societies that have spread throughout the world. One may be a citizen of any country and follow any religion, yet first and foremost, one is a human being. This is an identity beyond race or religion. In different societies, different kinds of people and classes can be seen, nonetheless they all have one aim and work: to uplift society and promote the welfare of society.

Those who try to organize society through authority and justice form the political class. Those who impart knowledge and skills for self-reliance, independence and autonomy, form the teaching class. Those who render service in the field of health belong to the medical class. Those who contribute towards construction and building are engineers. Those who teach internal discipline, restraint, appropriateness, peace and culture are known as *sadhus*, good or virtuous people, sages or saints.

Just as doctors, priests, businessmen and engineers have their own communities, sadhus and saints also have their community. This community has just one task: to promote the path of peace in society and spread spiritual culture. From this perspective, the sadhu is also an integral part of society and completes it. Nowadays, there are so many allegations that sadhus rob and cheat people, but this is a misconception. A sadhu does not demand millions of dollars from you; all he asks for is one or two rotis and one or two dhotis. What about those who misappropriate millions? A sadhu's duty is not to rob people, but to realize spirituality in his own life and guide others on the path.

Swami Sivananda's life of sacrifice

Paramguru Swami Sivananda was a venerated doctor who held an FRCS degree, a rare accomplishment in those days. He worked for some time in Malaysia, and one day he met a sadhu there. The sadhu gave him a book titled *Brahma Vichara*, meaning 'Contemplation of Brahma'. It is a small book, only about one hundred pages long, but it expresses the basic beliefs of the spiritual philosophy of India.

On reading the book, Swami Sivananda experienced an unexpected, blissful change in his mind and thinking. He gave up his field of work and returned to India. He got off the ship at Chennai and called one of his friends to deliver his luggage home, where he himself would not be returning. Swami Sivananda said, "I am not going home. I am going to the Himalayas in search of my guru and God." He boarded a train and started towards North India. On reaching there, he wandered about in search of his guru. He went to Allahabad, Benaras, Pandharpur and other such places of pilgrimage, reaching Rishikesh at the end. There he met a number of saints, yet did not find his guru.

One day in the afternoon, when he was resting under the shade of a tree and thinking about where or how he would find his guru, he felt a shadow over his closed eyes. He opened his eyes to see a sannyasin standing before him. The sannyasin asked, "Why are you sitting under this tree?" Swami Sivananda said, "I was thinking about where I will find my guru." The sannyasin said, "I am your guru, I will initiate you into sannyasa now."

In ten minutes, following all the rules and conventions, he initiated Swami Sivananda into sannyasa giving him the name of Swami Sivananda Saraswati. Only revealing that his name was Swami Vishwananda Saraswati, the sannyasin left. The meeting between guru and disciple lasted for only fifteen

to twenty minutes. In this short meeting, Swami Sivananda received initiation into sannyasa, and the spark of spirituality ignited inside him.

When the stick is dry it catches fire quickly, and when the stick is wet it only gives out smoke. The person engrossed in the world of maya is steeped in attraction and attachment, and is like a wet stick. No matter how much you try to burn it, it only gives out smoke. However, the one detached from the world of the senses and sense objects is like a dry stick, which can be lit with just one matchstick. Swami Sivananda was a dry stick, as he had left everything. He had just one thought, 'How do I attain higher experiences so I can contribute towards uplifting others?' The brief encounter with his guru was sufficient for the guru's energy to descend into Swami Sivananda and to set him on the path of sannyasa.

Spiritual obstacles

Swami Sivananda understood that the ultimate aim in life is to bring joy and happiness into the lives of others. He devised a plan to do this through *seva* or service, yoga practice and sadhana, and *atma chintan*, reflection on what one can do to become better and improve one's environment. In this process, Swami Sivananda outlines the obstacles faced in the cultivation of spiritual awareness.

He advises, "First you must know the obstacles in spiritual life, and then carefully stay away from them." You will keep yourself away from your enemies when you recognize them. If you do not even know who your enemy is, how will you save yourself from attack? What are the enemies, the obstacles in spiritual life? Swami Sivananda says the biggest enemy is the state of duality, which is maya. Then there is ego, vanity, the fear of death, pride, conceit, attraction-repulsion, arrogance, desire and sensuality, and big-headedness. He says multiplicity and plurality are also obstacles as they become the cause of mental distraction and diversion. The slave mentality, *ahamkara-ity*, the ego, sensitivity, sentimentality and inactivity are also obstacles on the path of spirituality. In this way, he identifies the obstacles faced in spiritual life that impede the attainment of divinity, universality and the real unity of self.

Swami Sivananda says that one outcome of duality is a fat head, meaning an inflated ego, and with this the mind's ability to grasp things comes to an end. If the body is overweight, there are difficulties in walking and moving about. In the same way, when you have a big, fat ego, it is difficult to be spontaneous and fluid. The mind becomes as rigid as a rock.

Be aware of these obstacles and be like a river when meeting with them. What is the nature of a river? It always flows down and never confronts an obstacle directly; it flows around it or over it. It does not come into conflict with the obstacle; it accepts the obstacle since it is there. It knows that by fighting the obstacle, nothing is going to change, and it is better to live life happily. Therefore, just flow around it, the obstacle will be left behind and the journey will continue. Have an aim that you are not going to struggle against the negative tendencies that can manifest, instead you will simply flow around them and continue with your journey.

Spiritual diary

There should be an awareness of all these obstacles. Begin by making a list of the obstacles you want to become vigilant towards. This can take the form of a spiritual diary that should be reviewed on a regular basis. It can be used to determine if you are alert to the spiritual obstacles or not, and if you are able to withstand the situations in which the obstacles arise.

In this way, go through the process of self-awareness and self-examination. When you gain knowledge about yourself, when you get to know your personality, nature, behaviour and conduct, you will try to overcome your weaknesses and adopt positive qualities, and your life will start becoming divine.

Swami Sivananda has explained in a simple manner what the sadhana of life should be, through which spirituality, purity, divinity and higher experiences become a part of one's life. Swami Sivananda says that through the constant and steady practice of yoga, you free yourself from mental and physical weaknesses and frailties. Connect yourself with the Supreme Element through worship and prayer, meditation, faith, devotion, self-confidence and willpower. When Swami Sivananda attained mahasamadhi, his last words were, "God is the only truth in this world." After uttering this last sentence he left his body; he had truly attained this highest experience and understanding in his life.

Purifying the emotions

Swami Sivananda says, "When I see any woman, I believe her to be the form of Devi and I mentally bow to her. I greet her by mentally saying the mantras, *Om Durgayai Namah*, *Om Saraswatyai Namah* and *Om Lakshmyai Namah*. I give her the status of Devi and I receive her blessings. When I see a man in front of me, I greet him as a Devata. 'You are Narayana,

you are Shiva,' is the feeling I have in my mind. Saying *Om Namah Shivaya, Om Namo Narayana*, I mentally bow to him, and accept his blessings." These are the words of Swami Sivananda. He does not say, "I give them my blessings." Instead, he says, "After greeting, I accept their blessings." Swami Sivananda actually lived this principle in his life.

There have been several incidents in his life that prove that after attaining a state of purity, God's energy always stays with such a being like a shadow. Before building the ashram in Rishikesh, Swami Sivananda used to live in a hut on the other side of the Ganga. There were other huts next to his that were inhabited by sadhus and sannyasins engaged in sadhana, satsang and self-study. During the evening, while going on a stroll they would talk to each other. Once, when the time of Navaratri was approaching, a sadhu who was

Swami Sivananda's neighbour said, "I wish to conduct the worship of the Divine Mother with full ornamentation, of jewels, clothes, fruits and flowers, but I am a fakir and I do not have any disciples. What to do?" He said this in jest and Swami Sivananda quietly listened.

Some days went by, and everyone forgot about what he had said. One day, while this swami was performing his sadhana, he heard a knock on the door of his hut. When he opened the door, he saw three Punjabi girls standing there with plates full of worship objects in their hands. The sadhu asked them, "Where have you come from, what is all this?" The girls said, "Swami Sivananda has sent them. You had expressed the desire to worship the Divine Mother with pomp and grandeur, so Swami Sivananda has made all the arrangements and sent all these articles for you." The sadhu thought that perhaps Swami Sivananda had told one of his wealthy devotees who complied with the articles. He accepted the articles.

When he met Swami Sivananda in the evening, he said, "Mahatma, thank you." Swami Sivananda asked, "Thank you for what?" He replied, "For the articles you sent for the worship of the Divine Mother." Swami Sivananda responded, "I didn't send anything to you." He said, "Swamiji, the three Punjabi girls who had come said you had sent it." The sadhu made enquiries in alms-houses and ashrams, but there was no trace of the three girls.

A number of years after Swami Sivananda's mahasamadhi, this sadhu came to the ashram and related the story to the sannyasins there. He said, "He was a true devotee and sadhaka. I had only expressed my desire before him, but when one whose feelings and mind are pure thinks of something, God himself hastens to fulfil his wish. This is the highest degree of faith and devotion."

While austerity and sadhana constitute the first path to awaken spirituality, faith, devotion, prayer and worship constitute the second, as they purify the emotions. This applies to both householders and sadhus. The only difference is that a householder's prayer is with desire, while a sadhu's prayer is without desire. A householder prays for the fulfilment of personal desires, whereas a sadhu prays for everyone. The power of a sadhu's prayer becomes many times more potent. This is the result of renunciation and a state of mind that is free of desires, a selfless state.

Eighteen ITIES of spiritual life

Swami Sivananda says that one must try to attain the qualities that will make your life disciplined, systematic and positive. Until you discipline your life, it is not possible to be free of the state of duality. Indiscipline will always pull you back into duality, whereas discipline will give you control over your mind. You must watch out for the traits that bind you and not free you.

You can strengthen your positive nature and will by cultivating certain specific qualities, disciplines and rules. Swami Sivananda has identified eighteen of these, known as the 'Eighteen ITIES'. These are: serenity, regularity, absence of vanity, sincerity, simplicity, veracity, equanimity, fixity, non-irritability, adaptability, humility, tenacity, integrity, nobility, magnanimity, charity, generosity, and purity. He identifies the eighteen qualities that can be cultivated to make life divine. These qualities can be cultivated in the form of yamas and niyamas, since ultimately it is the mind that requires transformation. The only way to change the quality of the mind is by working through yamas and niyamas, as they are the tools that change the perceptions of the mind.

In order to discipline your life, the first rule is to keep your mind established in serenity. Do not let the mind vacillate one way or the other. There should be no sign of excessive happiness or sadness on the face. It has been described in the *Ramacharitamanas* that when Sri Rama learnt that he was to be crowned king, he smiled. When he came to know that he had been exiled, he again smiled. If you were given such news, would you smile? No. One whose mind is still will have a serene nature. Make your mind still and become serene;

this is the first discipline. Serenity has been called mental austerity by Sri Krishna in the *Bhagavad Gita* (17:16):

> *Manah prasaadah saumyatvam maunamaatmavinigrahah;*
> *Bhaava samshuddhirityetattapo maanasamuchyate.*
>
> Cheerfulness of mind, serenity, habit of contemplation on God, control of the mind and perfect purity of inner feeling – all this is called austerity of the mind.

The second discipline is regularity. Only by regularity are the body, mind, emotions and spirit nourished. You eat at a specific time rather than eating randomly throughout the day. There is a time for breakfast, lunch and dinner. Eating at that specific time makes it easy to digest the food, for the body responds well to such habits. Similarly, the mind becomes healthy, happy and peaceful when it receives a few guidelines.

Swami Sivananda has elucidated these eighteen points to nurture the divine life. Maintain a feeling of serenity, follow regularity, and try to be free of arrogance and pride. Make a solemn promise to live life without deceit and with simplicity, practise truthful conduct, and maintain the feeling of equality. Become focused and concentrated, eradicate irritability from your life, behave well, and be humble. Be firm in decisions, become a person of integrity, be polite, be generous, be magnanimous, be charitable, and finally, be pure.

These eighteen reflections regulate and discipline human life. This frees one from what Swami Sivananda identifies as the negative 'ITIES' or traits to guard against: 'avidity' or greed, 'cupidity' or desire, 'stupidity' or delusion, 'audacity' or arrogance, 'turbidity' or confusion, 'instability' or wandering of the mind, 'angularity' or vanity, 'eccentricity' or whims, 'irritability' or anger in all its forms. The restraints and rules of the eighteen ITIES are applicable to everyone, whether one is a householder or a sannyasin, as through these the positive, divine, luminous aspects of consciousness can emerge.

There are four layers of the mind: *manas*, the rational mind; *buddhi*, the intellect; *chitta*, memories; and *ahamkara*, the ego. The dissipated state of these four layers gives rise to dissipated patterns in the awareness. The *Yoga Sutras* say (1:2): *Yogaschitta vritti nirodhah* – "To block the patterns of consciousness is yoga." The only way to gain peace is by blocking the vrittis. This is a discipline, a sadhana, and a process through which you will free yourself from the negative, detrimental results of duality, and this has been the teaching of Swami Sivananda. Up to this point, there is a similarity in the path of the householder and the sannyasin.

There is a trick in this sutra. One thinks that stopping the *chitta vrittis*, the modifications of the mind, is the aim of yoga; however, this idea and concept does not give the complete understanding of yoga. Stopping the chitta vrittis is not yoga; rather, the creation of a sixth mental state is the purpose of yoga. One has to make the effort to give birth to a sixth vritti. If this sixth vritti is able to emerge, it will overpower all the other five. The *Yoga Sutras* define five kinds of vrittis which connect one to the external world: *pramana*, right knowledge; *viparyaya*, wrong knowledge; *vikalpa*, fantasy; *nidra*, sleep; and *smriti*, memory.

When you move from the material to the spiritual, you do not have to fight against these five existing vrittis. You are a single person and they are five powerful forces. You will never be victorious. Instead, give birth to a protector. The protector is another vritti known as *brahmi vritti*, the transcendental, divine vritti. The brahmi vritti represents a state of existence in which purity and harmony are the foundations of nature and personality. Where purity and harmony become the foundation of the personality, you live a divine life. These eighteen ITIES given by Swami Sivananda aid in the development, generation and awakening of a new brahmi vritti that is more balanced, focused and aligned with spiritual aspirations. The brahmi vritti is the answer to the struggle with the five powerful vrittis already governing and ruling your life.

The eighteen yamas and niyamas become the tools to work with the mind. To deal with the stresses and anxieties of the dualistic mind and its six manifestations, there are the practices of pratyahara and dharana. Through these practices, you may observe and discover how intense the hold of passion and aggression is in your life and what you can do to modify and manage those influences. This is the subject of pratyahara and dharana: to manage the existing condition. To give birth to a new condition, however, is the subject of yamas and niyamas. Therefore, do not ignore the yamas and niyamas as simply moral or ethical teachings of yoga. This may be your understanding. Yoga does not preach ethics or morality; it is about the quality of mind that you can have: a mind that lets you lead a divine life.

The result of meditation and worship is happiness and peace, and it is not obtained from outside; it exists within you.

The person who makes the effort to attain this happiness, peace and freedom from the negative consequences of the state of duality is called a seeker. A seeker's efforts lead him to experience changes in the mental behaviour and the expressions of emotion. The mind connects with God instead of worldly matters. This disciplined mind is purified further through higher sadhana. The disciplines, restraints and rules bring about a positive mental change and redirect the materialistic mind towards spirituality.

Culmination of spiritual life

The yogic philosophy says that a person is never free from the mind. Even in the state of samadhi, the mind remains aware, wakeful and active. When the mind is awake in this state, what kind of behaviour and form does it assume? Right now, the mind is object-oriented. In the state of samadhi, the mind does not remain object-oriented. The worldly vritti changes into a divine vritti. The vrittis are never destroyed; they simply change into a transcendental vritti.

When the worldly conditions that influence and affect you by causing happiness and unhappiness transform and transmute, you become free from worldly happiness and unhappiness and live in divine awareness. When this divine awareness awakens internally, you become like a flute.

Once, Radha said to Krishna, "Krishna, it seems that your flute is dearer to you than me." Krishna replied, "Yes, Radha, you are right. This flute is definitely very dear to me." Radha asked, "Why?" Krishna replied, "Because it is hollow from within, it is empty; there is nothing inside." When a musician plays a hollow flute, it produces a beautiful, sweet melody. When Krishna plays the hollow flute, every creature is held under its spell and begins to dance. Similarly, when you become empty of the tamasic vrittis and your materialistic mind transforms into a spiritual mind, then God's divine, transcendental music can flow through you. This is spirituality.

Teachings of Vedanta

Morning, 7 March 2013

The vedic civilization of India gave birth to many sects, philosophies and religions. Faith in God and belief in one's self have been the foundation of this civilization. The sages and saints were able to reach and experience high states of realization on the basis of this faith and belief. They had deep insights into how human beings can attain fullness, happiness and satisfaction in their lives. The seers then shared their revelations, thoughts and realizations to form what is now known as Vedanta.

There is just one thread in the Vedanta philosophy: "There is one God, not two." There is one God or Supreme Element, and nothing else besides that. The vedic seers saw the reflection and the light of this Supreme Element in every being, in every atom of creation. In the *Ramacharitamanas,* Sri Tulsidas has expressed this sentiment as: *Siyaramamaya saba jaga jani, karau pranama jori juga pani* – "The whole world as Sita-Rama I know; with folded hands to you I bow."

This basic principle of the sanatana dharma rests on faith and belief. You experience the all-pervasiveness of God on the strength of faith and belief. God is all-pervasive, He exists inside every atom, and to discover this is a human being's primary goal. Swami Sivananda says the aim of human life is attaining God. Is this possible? With your limited brain, how will you know the endless Supreme Spirit, how will you grasp it? How will you think about something that is inconceivable?

He says there is only one way to know and understand the inconceivable and the unknown: increase your capacity. In order to experience the unlimited, you need to expend the boundaries of your limited mind and make it all-pervasive. As the mind becomes expansive, it no longer remains isolated. When your mind is not isolated, then the experience of God is not far from you.

Residence of God

Sri Swamiji says that you have forgotten that God is closest to you, closer than your breath, thoughts and ideas. Having forgotten this truth, you are looking for God outside when actually He is within you. He is inside you and you are His reflection or image that acts out a role in this world. When you are playing this role, you forget that this is just an act, and you start viewing yourself as the actor or doer, forgetting your real identity with the Supreme Self.

It is like when you go to the cinema to see a movie, and seeing a sad scene, you start crying, or while watching another scene you become angry. You are not actually a part of the movie, you are only a witness. You are not even acting in the movie, you are sitting quietly and watching the images on the screen, and you cry and laugh, feel angry and frightened, for you identify with the actors, the performance and the story while you are witnessing the movie.

Just as you cry seeing a sad scene in the cinema, will not God sitting within you cry seeing your depressed state? Just as you sit in the theatre, God is sitting as a witness within every person. These are the words of Sri Swamiji. God sitting within is not disconnected from the happiness and sadness experienced by an individual. If you experience unhappiness in your life, then you are not experiencing this alone; along with you God is also experiencing it. If you experience happiness in your life, then it is not only you who laughs, God sitting within you also laughs and feels happy, since He is present within you in the form of your soul.

The soul within you is a part of God; it is like a reflection. When you establish a relationship with the soul within, you receive spiritual strength from it. Through intellectual skill, you acquire knowledge and the art of living. You go to school and college to study, acquire a degree, start working. All this is a result of intellectual ability. If there is no intellectual ability, learning has no meaning. Learning awakens your intellect and teaches you the art of living. In the same way, when you establish a relationship with your soul, the strength that you receive is spiritual energy, which is able to drive away all difficulties in life.

God's blessings

Once, a sage started performing austerities with the desire to receive the darshan of God. At the end of the austerities, God appeared and said, "I have come. Ask for a boon." Completely overcome, the sage fell at God's feet and said, "My sadhana has fructified, I have received your darshan, Lord. The desire and aim with which I had undertaken this sadhana has been realized. I have nothing more to ask of you. I am fulfilled and content."

God said, "Well, I vowed to give you something, so you must ask for a boon." The sadhu said, "God, you know my heart. You know I do not want anything, why are you telling me again and again to ask for a boon?" God thought, 'What do I do? Whenever I manifest before someone, they always want something or the other from me. That is why the first sentence that comes out of my mouth is, "Ask for a boon", so we do not waste too much time in formalities.'

What God said is true. Whenever He comes near you, you do ask for something or the other. The sage said, "God, really, I don't want anything. Don't make fun of my devotion by giving me something." He bowed and turning his back on God, started walking away. God was rather impressed by this devotee. He stood there thinking, 'What kind of a devotee is this? Until today, whenever I have come to earth, whether on account of a human being, a demon, a god, or a saint, everyone has asked me for something or the other. This is the first person turning his back on me and rejecting my boon, as his purpose is fulfilled. He only wanted my darshan. Nonetheless, I am also bound by my promise. What shall I do?'

While God was thinking about this, his glance fell on the shadow of the sage. He blessed the sage's shadow with the ability to rejuvenate whatever it fell upon. The sadhu had no awareness of this; he continued walking, revelling in his happiness. He was lost in bliss for having received the darshan of God. Behind the sadhu, however, his shadow was working miracles. If his shadow fell upon a shrivelled, dried-up tree, the tree became green and laden. If the shadow fell upon a blind man, he regained his sight. If the shadow fell upon a leper, his skin became smooth once again. If his shadow fell upon a dead body, it came back to life.

The sage knew none of this and therefore he remained completely natural, simple and humble. That is why when God gives blessings, He does not tell you that He is doing so. His blessings bring happiness and auspiciousness into your life in mysterious yet natural ways.

Kingdom of maya

In order to experience God and his blessings, you must first go through the kingdom of maya. Maya starts with the state of duality, and where maya reigns, all the tamasic qualities take birth. The transformation of this state will happen when you are able to plant positive seeds on the ground of your mind.

In one distant part of the country, one hard-working man purchased a plot of land which was barren. Nothing grew on it except weeds and thorns. Through hard work and incessant effort, this man removed the thorns and the weeds, levelled the ground, cleared the soil, prepared the earth and planted seeds of flowering and fruit trees. After a few years, when the garden blossomed, it was recognized as the most beautiful garden in the country. People came from everywhere to see it. One day, hearing about its fame, a priest visited the garden. Stunned by the beauty of everything around him, he exclaimed, "Look at this creation of God! Isn't it wonderful?" The gardener heard him and replied, "No, sir, this is not God's creation. This is my creation. This is the outcome of my hard work. I have planted the flowers. I have planted the seeds. I have taken care of everything, and you are saying this is God's creation? You should have seen this patch of land when God owned it. Nothing used to grow here. It was barren, except for thorns and weeds."

The nature of prakriti is tamasic, and it has great strength. If you do not look after your land, what will happen? In ten years' time no flowers or fruit will grow there, only weeds.

In this body, personality and life, have you ever learned how to be envious, greedy, jealous, negative, hateful and angry? Nobody has taught you; all these tendencies come up naturally, they don't require any learning. This indicates that the nature of prakriti is negative and tamasic. The nature of the mind is also tamasic. Every person wants to know how to practise devotion, how to become more loving, compassionate and sensitive. Why are these not natural virtues? This is due to the tamoguna in the mind.

If you ask an actor which role is easier, the good guy or the bad guy, he will say that it is easy and natural to play a bad character, but difficult to play a virtuous, good person. It is the nature of the mind to express tamoguna easily, whereas to acquire sattwa guna you must work extra hard. This is the dual nature of the mind. Therefore, Sri Swamiji says that with this limited mind, how can you know the unlimited; how can you experience non-duality in the mind whose nature is duality?

Sadhana to attain non-duality

Swami Sivananda says that it is through the process of sadhana that the mind is mastered, and made pure and divine. The sadhana that he speaks about is not austerity; it is a method and process of mastering the mind, and includes eight steps.

First, the mind must be cleared of the influence of tamas, and *shuddhi*, purity, attained. Second, the mind should be able to focus and concentrate so the mental dissipations are reduced. Third, one should be able to reflect, not just react. Instead of reacting, discrimination should be cultivated through reflection. Fourth is the ability to meditate; through meditation, one should connect with the faculty of discrimination to conquer desires and weaknesses. Fifth is self-knowledge to discover one's own self and connect with one's positive qualities, rather than the negative aspects of the personality. Sixth, to identify not with the sense objects, the environment or people, but with one's inner self that is free from every kind of influence. It is the mind that is influenced, not the soul or the spirit. Therefore, identify with the spirit and observe the mind like a parent observes the play of the child. When you become absorbed in that identity of the spirit, you attain liberation and freedom from the bondage of duality. Therefore, purification, concentration, reflection, meditation, illumination, identification, absorption, salvation: these are the eight steps in spiritual sadhana.

One of the greatest efforts in spiritual sadhana is the management of the ego. How will the negative, destructive, hard shell of the ego be destroyed? Swami Sivananda used to sing a song:

Within you is the hidden God.
Within you is the immortal soul.
Kill this little 'i'. Die to live.
Lead the divine life.
Within you is the fountain of joy.
Rest peacefully in your own atman.
Drink the nectar of immortality.

"Kill this little 'i', die to live, lead the divine life." It is this 'little i', the ego, which confuses and confounds you. It creates different images that you perceive as your personal self-image, and when there is a threat to this personal self-image, one feels fear and insecurity. There are three methods to destroy or modify the negative ego: sacrifice, surrender, and *sanyam*, restraint.

Sacrifice: The meaning of self-sacrifice is not terminating your own existence; instead, the negative traits of the mind, the six enemies of the mind have to be sacrificed. You have to become free from the influences of the six enemies of lust, anger, greed, infatuation, arrogance and jealousy, since they drag you down to the depths of hell when they are intense. You must rise above the state of selfishness and develop the state of selflessness where you sacrifice yourself for uplifting others. Freedom from the selfish tendencies and patterns created by the six enemies is a state of sacrifice.

These six enemies are considered selfish as they only want to accomplish their purpose, nothing beyond that. Selfishness is prominent in the state of duality, and selflessness is established only when you rise above the state of duality and experience unity. Only then are you able to connect with others, and see the reflection of the divine spark, the universal spirit in others. True self-sacrifice is to free yourself from all the bonds of selfishness created by lust, anger, greed, infatuation, arrogance and jealousy, and to sacrifice your selfishness.

Surrender: The second way to destroy the hard ego is by self-surrender. Surrender is to the divine will: 'Let Thy will be done.' As long as the ego predominates with the idea remaining in the mind that 'I am the centre of my action', 'I am the doer', 'I am the performer' and 'I am the enjoyer', there is suffering, pain, elation, pleasure, depression and anxiety. As long as the hard ego exists, there is identification with both the doer and the enjoyer. When you identify yourself as the doer, your mind is always attached to the material world of the senses and sense objects, not with the soul and God. To develop surrender there has to be acceptance and adjustment: to accept the situations of life as they come, as you accept the weather. Whether it is hot or cold, you adjust with the conditions. If need be, you put on some more layers of clothing. If need be, you turn on the heater. There is a process of adjustment, not denial.

In the same manner, in spiritual life there has to be a process of adjustment and not denial. This adjustment makes you accept the situations as and when they happen, since then you realize that you are not the doer or enjoyer; you are only an instrument through which the melody of a song is being played. The realization that a melody is being played through you is the state of surrender. If you are aware that the melody of the Supreme Spirit is being played through you, that is surrender, identification and oneness. This form of surrender lowers the scale of the ego; it brings it a notch lower.

One who connects with the Higher Self tries to transform every action into an action performed for the welfare of others, and every thought into a positive one. The awareness of and connection with God changes the behaviour of the person. When there is a relationship with God, the feeling of doership and enjoyership reduces, instead the feeling emerges that 'I am not the doer nor am I the enjoyer.' When you are not the doer or the enjoyer, then who is the doer and who is the enjoyer? You will say, "The spirit, the God within me is the only doer and only enjoyer. The body and mind are just mediums, in reality I am the spirit." In this state there is balance and equanimity in both happiness and unhappiness. This is the real form of surrender.

Sanyam: The third point is sanyam, restraint, which gives birth to a better understanding and awareness of one's actions and reactions. Restraint helps you discriminate and analyze what you actually need, and what is only a desire. By gradually lessening the pull of desire in your life through sanyam, you attain happiness and peace, since lust, craving and desire are the cause of dissipation of the senses, mind and emotions. Restraint will discipline and focus the mind.

Thus, sacrifice, surrender and sanyam are the three methods to manage the ego, the 'I' identity. Sacrifice is cutting off all the strings of selfishness, surrender is surrendering to the will of God, and restraint is developing control and mastery. With these three you can destroy the ego. After managing the ego, the next stage of sadhana is something that makes you realize who you are, the means to self-understanding: self-analysis, self-introspection and self-examination, which take you to self-realization. This last level of sadhana is actually the state of dhyana, as you can go through this process only in the state of meditation. It is here that higher spiritual awakening is possible.

The process of sadhana starts with something gross and physical, material and basic: the attainment of purity. Through that process you come to the point of meditation where you discover and realize yourself. By following the stages of sadhana, you cultivate spiritual awareness, from one percent to fifty percent, and upon completion of the sadhana, when the spiritual attainments become a part of your expression in life, you become a sattwic, illumined person.

Goal of human life

Swami Satyananda says that the goal of human life is not God-realization or liberation. The purpose of human life is to awaken and cultivate spiritual awareness. When you gradually integrate these different methods of sadhana into your life, spiritual awareness will awaken and you will acquire sattwic qualities and virtues in your life.

When the process of purification, concentration and reflection is completed and sattwic virtues have been attained, certain traits and characteristics emerge which are expressed as spiritual ethics. Such people are bold, pure, wise, virtuous, honest, sincere, truthful, patient, tolerant, obedient, simple, humble, noble and gentle, for they can adapt, adjust and accommodate. They gain the strength to do the highest sadhana of life, which is to bear insult and bear injury. That is the ultimate test of the ego. If you can do this, your mind will never be disturbed. In the solitude and darkness of your room, you can say, "In meditation I have overcome my ego." However, this must be put into practice. Let somebody come and abuse you left, right, and centre. If you can keep smiling at that time, peacefully and joyously, then you can proclaim, "I have eradicated my ego."

Swami Sivananda says that this is the highest sadhana of life. Somebody who can bear insult and injury and remain equipoised and free from every kind of reactive, negative response is a pious and spiritual person. Every person wants to acquire a peaceful mind, yet how do you recognize a peaceful mind? According to Swami Sivananda, the sign of a peaceful mind is remaining undisturbed when you are scorned and insulted, to always remain happy. A person whose mind remains calm and undisturbed under scorn and insult has an awakened spiritual energy.

Difference between religion and spirituality

It is essential to know the difference between religion and spirituality, and to understand what spirituality is. Religion is a belief, a social system, a discipline, a faith and a ritual that connects the individual to God externally. Spirituality is the purification of life, which involves driving away tamasic influences and allowing the sattwic influences to grow. Spirituality is removing the impurities and negative influences to attain the state of purity; it is the process of becoming free from negative habits and patterns, and allowing the flowers of positive qualities to blossom in life.

Spirituality is the subject of sadhana and religion is that of tradition. The tradition passed on from one generation to another is the expression of religion. Spirituality, however, is a personal effort and sadhana to bring peace, fullness, simplicity, humility and purity into life. Without spirituality, you cannot realize religion. The purpose of religion should be to take you towards spirituality, by which you can experience inner purity and balance, and can express faith, love and compassion. This is the teaching of Vedanta.

Vedanta is a powerful tradition of India. It is a school of thought which emphasizes the awareness of a higher reality while living your life in the world, a balance between spiritual awareness and material awareness. People say that Vedanta is only philosophy; however, the sages, saints and sannyasins across the ages have provided practical methods of applying these philosophies and traditions in life, keeping with the times and context. Included in this list of luminaries are Swami Sivananda and Swami Satyananda who have both given practical methods of applying spiritual principles in life.

The Vedanta philosophy can be lived in a practical way; however, one should also have the desire to grow on that path, as this is a teaching on how to transform one's life. Vedanta is the process by which you can rise above the attraction for the material world and establish yourself in spiritual experience. The obstacles, sadhanas and conditions that Swami Sivananda has spoken of are to realize this vedantic way of thinking.

If you want to become a doctor, you have to start studying the related subjects in school. You have to learn biology, physics and other sciences. Gradually, after a long period of study, you become a doctor. Similarly, to awaken spiritual awareness, you cannot fight with the mind or suppress it. You must have knowledge of all the aspects of the mind that keep it bound to the senses, sense objects and material life; you must have knowledge of its capacity, ability, strengths and weaknesses. Only then will you gain victory over it.

Mantra sadhana to develop a divine mind

To develop the spiritual vritti, one method given by Swami Sivananda is mantra sadhana. Generally, people think that in order to chant mantra, many rules and regulations must be followed and one must become someone's disciple. It is up to you if you want to become a disciple or not. Irrespective, the tool of mantra nourishes the mind and the spirit.

At the time of mantra chanting, while remaining in the state duality, you are repeating the names and qualities of the Supreme Spirit, of God. You are thinking of God and remembering His divine qualities. There is awareness of three things in mantra sadhana: mantra, form and qualities. If you are chanting *Om Namah Shivaya*, then the form seen in the mind is that of Shiva, not Vishnu, Brahma, Agni, Indra or Varuna. Along with the mantra there is a form which appears in the mind. When the form is seen, you also begin to know the qualities of that form. What is the quality of Shiva? What is the quality of Narayana, Rama or Devi? When the form appears before the mind, you will know their particular qualities that bestow peace and happiness, and assist you in liberating yourself from the difficulties of life. These qualities will help you in developing inner strength and conviction to overcome the limitations of life, and see your circumstances in a positive light.

In the beginning stages of mantra sadhana, it is necessary to first still the body, sit quietly while holding the mala. After steadiness of the body has been achieved, you begin to chant the mantra and meditate on the chosen form of the divine, the *ishta*, and the qualities associated with that form. In the course of time, as your proficiency in mantra sadhana develops, you will find that it is not necessary to sit down or even use a mala for doing mantra japa, as the mantra repeats in the mind automatically. The mantra that you have chanted for a few malas daily repeats effortlessly, easily and naturally in the mind. Sometimes you think, 'I do not even know for how long this mantra has been playing in my mind.' When you wake up in the morning, you may become aware that you were chanting the mantra even in your sleep. Thus, the gross sadhana is having an effect at the subtle level. After some time, due to the effects of the mantra, your perspective changes. When you look at someone and the mantra *Om Namah Shivaya* is going on in your mind, you can see the form of the divine, the qualities of the ishta, in the other person. This is the result of mantra sadhana. It is not only sannyasins who have such realizations, householder aspirants have also experienced this.

In this manner, when the mantra has a hold on the mind, the inner mind awakens and spiritual awareness is developed. Therefore, mantra sadhana is considered mandatory for every person who wants to cultivate spiritual awareness. In the Indian culture, mantra sadhana is given great importance in the guru-disciple tradition. The disciple wants freedom from suffering and difficulties in life, and he receives a mantra from the guru. The relationship between a guru and his disciple is that of mantra, as it is through the mantra that the guru transfers his spiritual energy. It is through the energy of the mantra that there is an awakening of spiritual awareness in the disciple which first connects him to divinity. When the individual connects with the ishta, the reflection of the ishta is seen in the world. Thus the disciple becomes humble and bows down before the world. The tamasic and narrow way of thinking changes and the mind becomes full of positive, sattwic, pure and divine thoughts. This transformation of the mind affects one's expressions so that the individual is inspired to express a positive, sattwic behaviour in life.

For an ordinary individual, this is the journey of spirituality. When one becomes pure in thought, lives a disciplined spiritual lifestyle and expresses a positive behaviour, then the kingdom of heaven is achieved in this life itself. One becomes free from all affliction, suffering, difficulty, tension and disturbance. One then lives in this world like a lotus in water, blooming on the surface of the water, yet remaining dry and unaffected by the mud in the water.

This is the most important teaching of Vedanta: to realize the experience of the invisible, infinite, unperceivable and unknowable, the highest reality. When you look at the lives of saints, the practical application of this philosophy becomes perceptible. An individual becomes a saint not when they have had realization of the Supreme Spirit, but when that high state of experience transforms their entire mind. They become established in that exalted level of consciousness and live by it, conducting their life with discipline and dedication.

If an individual is unable to turn a thought or an idea into behaviour, and only says, "Ah, this is a good idea and philosophy, but I can't do it", that person is called a *dhela*, a lump of earth. You can throw a lump of earth and it will stay where it falls for years. The person who has to be reminded time and again, "You can do better, you have that capacity, strength and ability", and who has to be encouraged again and again is called a *thela*, a pushcart, as you have to keep pushing it to move to the next destination. The person who imbibes the teachings and lives according to them is a *chela*, a disciple. If you want to be useless, be a dhela. If you want to move forward and develop by laughing, crying, falling and stumbling, become a thela. If you want to excel, become a chela. The choice is yours.

A Spiritual Lifestyle

Afternoon, 7 March 2013

According to Sri Swami Satyananda, the purpose of life is not God-realization or self-realization; it is the cultivation of spiritual awareness. How far you go depends on you, but you have to start the journey. It is like going to school, and moving from one class to the next each year until you complete the academic journey. In the same manner, in spiritual life you begin your journey with the cultivation of an awareness that is different from the material, sensorial, sensual and gross awareness. The aspect that is different from the sensorial, gross and material experience can be tapped to become a resource for success, contentment, fulfilment, happiness and joy in life, and can give the ability and the resilience to manage the struggles, strife, pain and suffering with a balanced mind.

Spirituality in this context is the process of purification that drives out inner disturbances and brings inner peace. The attainment of peace results in happiness and fulfilment in life. This happiness and fulfilment takes place on various levels; it is not just material, it is also mental, emotional and spiritual. When spirituality dawns, every act is filled with happiness, contentment and peace; there is understanding in every interaction in life.

After developing this level of divinity in the personality and conduct, you are free to walk whichever path you wish. If you walk the path of worldly life, you will be a virtuous, good, sattwic person and will inspire respect, love and cooperation. If you walk the path of renunciation, then the peace in your life will give you the experience of the highest element. Whichever path you choose, whether that of senses and sense objects, or the dimension of the spirit, you will be successful.

Evolution is continuous; every soul evolves with each birth. Evolution provides the possibility of realizing fullness. In the Vedas it is said that life and nature are created out of fullness, live in fullness and die in fullness. Thus, fullness is the destiny of the soul.

End of suffering

Spirituality is a process of attaining inner purity, harmony, peace and contentment, through modification and transformation of the behaviours and attitudes that split the personality. Tension splits the personality; worries split the personality. For whatever reason, perhaps due to stress, illness, or imbalance, tension becomes the cause of a fractured personality. This fractured personality becomes the centre of problems, difficulties and illnesses.

The ancient scriptures do not speak of God-realization; they show the way to eradicate pain and suffering. The tantras do not speak of God-realization; they speak of finding a solution to problems, difficulties, pain and suffering in life. The Samkhya school of thought does not speak of God-realization; it speaks of finding solutions to the conflicts in life. The vedic tradition does not speak of God-realization; it is concerned with finding solutions to the difficulties of life. When the Buddha started his journey, he had three questions in mind: 'What is pain?' 'From where does it come?' 'How can we overcome suffering and pain?' These three questions propelled him in his spiritual journey. Lord Mahavir, the founder of the Jain school of thought, started his spiritual quest with the desire to understand the cause of pain and suffering and how to alleviate them. The founders of various traditions, religions, philosophies and schools of thought came up with particular philosophies or sadhanas to eradicate suffering in life.

In the tantra shastras, Mother Parvati asks Lord Shiva, "There is so much suffering in the world; are humans born only to bear suffering?" Shiva says, "No, the world is not a house of suffering. It is a training centre where the human being finds himself in various circumstances and conditions and tries to rise above these. When there is unhappiness, disease and distress in life, freedom from these conditions is sought. As one finds freedom from suffering and distress, there is growth and expansion; one becomes capable and competent, and develops faith, belief and inner strength."

Mother Parvati further asks, "Lord, how many kinds of suffering are there and what are the methods to be free of them?" Lord Shiva now imparts the teachings of tantra. The subject of tantra is not connected to God-realization. People interpret it like that; however, the real purpose of the philosophy and sadhanas of tantra is eradication of suffering from human life. In the same way, in Samkhya darshan, Sage Kapila was asked by his mother, "Where is happiness in this world? You can see nothing but suffering in all four directions here." In response, Sage Kapila tells his mother the philosophy of Samkhya to alleviate suffering.

This indicates that Indian philosophy is not alienated from life. It teaches how human life can be lived in the best possible manner; how to gain freedom from suffering, distress, worry and trouble, and live a peaceful, happy life. When you begin to walk the path of sadhana, then the guru gives guidance to show a way to endure and manage the duality of mind. The guru gives a direction to the mind: to concentrate the mind on the Supreme Element which you call God.

Thus, while the traditions, religions, philosophies and schools of thought speak of eradication of suffering, gurus do not speak of the eradication of suffering in life; they speak of connecting with the divine source to realize the divine power. It seems that there is a contradiction between what

ND YOGA II ॐ
ND YOGA II ॐ
ND YOGA II ॐ

the scriptures say and what the gurus are saying, and this confuses the mind of the common person. However, if you attempt to analyze and understand these teachings, you will find they complement each other. The priority in life is not God-realization; it is learning how to manage life situations and conditions which can disturb your ease, comfort, peace and balance. Once this happens, the focus can shift to something different. The first priority is to find the comfort zone where the mind is at peace with itself and there are no cravings, expectations, desires or reactive nature, and instead a contented, joyous, fulfilled and happy nature predominates.

Pratipaksha bhavana: cultivating the opposite feeling

To weigh vegetables, you put vegetables on one tray of the scale and a weight on the other tray of the scale. If you want five kilos and you have put on weights totalling three kilos, you will put more. When the weight reaches five kilos, the scale will be balanced. If you put on another weight of five kilos, the weight tray will become heavy and go down and the vegetable tray will go up.

This principle can be used with the mind also. In your life there is both good and bad, negativity and positivity, luminosity and darkness, flaws and virtues. Put your negative actions, shortcomings and limitations on one side of the scale; and on the other side, pile up your positive actions and behaviours, your talents, strengths, capacities and good qualities. See which is heavier: the positive side or the negative side. If you want your good qualities to weigh heavier, you will pay attention to developing them. If you only attempt to eliminate the negative qualities, your attention will always be on them and you will never be able to cultivate your positive traits.

For this reason, you should pay attention to your good qualities and continue to enhance and cultivate them. The weight of the negative, destructive qualities of your personality will automatically lighten. In yoga, this is known as *pratipaksha bhavana*, cultivation of the opposite feeling. Observe and develop the opposite of what you are experiencing just now. If there is misery in your life, then do not identify with misery, instead cultivate happiness. If you are having hard, cruel thoughts, cultivate the feeling of kindness. The mind is the cause of restlessness, despondency and dissipation, and determines your behaviour in life. During times of sadness, link yourself with happiness; during struggle, bring to mind the source of inner strength. In this way, suffering is managed and peace and balance can be acquired in life. That is why the philosophies say that freedom from suffering is the karma of life and the guru says that connection with God is the dharma of life. The combination of the two helps you become a witness of your suffering and remain unaffected by it.

Classification of suffering

To eradicate suffering from life, you have to know what suffering is and what its causes are. The tradition has classified suffering in three groups: *adhidaivika* – suffering due to natural and divine causes; *adhibhautika* – suffering arising from the world; and *adhyatmika* – self-generated suffering. Earthquakes and natural disasters are adhidaivika, over which a person has no control. Bacterial, viral problems and infections are adhibhautika, generated by the world. Adhyatmika are sufferings that come up from within. To overcome the three categories of suffering, three different methods are to be used.

Adhidaivika: For calamities and natural disasters like earthquakes or floods, which you have no control over, it is the work of destiny. The way to deal these natural disasters and the problems arising out of them is to accept them, surrender yourself to God, flow with the current, and safeguard yourself as best as you can. Surrendering and safeguarding are the methods adopted to protect yourself from the suffering caused by natural disasters. Will you be able to stop an earthquake? No, you will have to accept it and also protect yourself based on the circumstances. Using the two methods of safeguard and surrender, one can take care of oneself during suffering caused by destiny.

Adhibhautika: This suffering relates to those external circumstances that create disease. You eat food and your stomach gets upset; you breathe in pollution and a problem develops in the lungs. If there is no discipline in life, high blood pressure can appear. If you cannot stop your greed and the craving of the tongue, diabetes occurs. These diseases are created by external circumstances and by germs and bacterial infections. To deal with these problems, the method is discipline and regularity in the daily routine. Yoga can be incorporated to manage these negative influences which affect your physical, psychological and spiritual health.

What is the meaning of discipline? There must be a fixed time for waking up, eating and sleeping that follows the laws and rhythms of nature. When the sun rises, the energies and internal clock in an individual awaken and when the sun sets, the energies become weak and dissipated. This is confirmed by science. Accordingly, in the Indian tradition it has always been a rule to take food between sunrise and sunset. This is a discipline, based on scientific understanding, that food must be eaten at the time when the pranas are awake. If your pranas are asleep and you eat food, you will fall ill.

Nowadays, many people eat at ten o'clock in the night and go to sleep at eleven o'clock, waking up in the morning with constipation, belching, gas, acidity and bile. They then approach the doctor for medicine. This is bound to happen, as it is a natural consequence of eating when the pranas of the body are asleep. When your pranas are asleep, the body

cannot effectively absorb nutritious food, and will succumb to illness.

When there is discipline in life, all this changes; the body and mind function properly. Digestion and respiration function soundly, the brain works well and becomes sharp; the senses gain strength and you acquire strength and ability. If discipline is absent, however, first your strength will be depleted and then the mind will become weak. Therefore, to eliminate suffering brought about by worldly life, engrossed in the senses and sense objects, discipline with routine and regular timings is essential. This will allow you to discipline all actions in your life. When all your actions are disciplined, good health is certain.

When you become ill, whether it is physical or mental illness, you need to find a way to be free from it. Modern medicine does not treat illness and disease; it treats the symptoms. If you get high blood pressure or asthma, or the muscles of the body become weak, these conditions affect the body from the inside. In such instances, yoga has a solution. The practice of yoga regulates the body, the pranas and the subtle energy. The theory of yoga says that a balance between *prana shakti*, vital life force, and *chitta shakti*, mental force, brings about good health.

When there is a balance between prana shakti and chitta shakti, the body's immunity to disease increases and it can then fight against any disease. If you train and discipline your body through yoga, then even if it is your destiny to have a fever for fifteen days, you will be fine in five days. If it is in your destiny that after a certain age you will have diabetes and suffer from it for the rest of your life, through yoga sadhana it may be possible that you can be free from it within a few months. In this way, by bringing discipline into life, it is possible to be free from the ill effects of suffering brought about by material causes.

Adhyatmika: The third kind of suffering springs from within oneself; it is self-generated. There are various mental conditions like tension, anxiety and worry. From these stem other problems like insomnia, amnesia, high blood pressure and a weak nervous system. When this situation continues, many more conditions can manifest. If you have malice, hatred or envy towards someone, then that mental illness can also result in high blood pressure, insomnia or loss of appetite; all the abilities and strengths of the body go on strike. Tension, worry and disturbances can all cause illness of the mind and become the reason that suffering is caused by oneself. This is the bane of most people today. There is tension at work, at home, in society, everywhere. You alone create this environment of stress in every direction. To remedy this situation, the mind needs to be improved. Managing the tension, stress and anxiety through meditation and yoga is the solution for adhyatmika suffering.

After remedying all these situations, one can become free from every kind of suffering. What happens then? When freedom from suffering has been achieved, fullness is experienced. Everyone has had an experience of fullness and contentment in certain situations where you feel that nothing more is needed. The thought comes to the mind, 'I am completely satisfied.' Sometimes you have this experience at a place of pilgrimage, when you feel totally happy and blissful. That one moment of satisfaction makes you say, 'I don't want anything else now.' What is the meaning of satisfaction? Fullness: I am full, I don't need anything else. The experience of contentment is what gives peace and bliss, and the way to be content is to reduce tension.

Sadhana and goal

The root of all three kinds of suffering is the state of duality. In duality, you see yourself as separate from every other living creature and take pride in your identity. This pride and arrogance keeps you under the spell of maya. By giving up the pride, you become free of the chains of maya. From time to time, whenever saints are born, they indicate the way to a spiritual lifestyle through which you may free yourself from the chains of maya.

The tradition and scriptures say that by following a specific process, discipline, system and sadhana, you can equip yourself to better manage the pain and suffering that come due to adhyatmika, adhidaivika or adhibhautika causes. Sadhus and gurus say that while you are learning how to deal with the sufferings, have a focus in mind. When dealing with the dualistic conditions, focus on the goal before you while you attempt to change and transform yourself. After all, you do not get on a train without a destination. If you get on the train, you need to buy the tickets in advance. If you are travelling from Munger to Delhi, the *lakshya*, the goal, is Delhi, although it takes many hours to get there. In those hours, you do not worry about when you will reach Delhi. Instead, you make yourself comfortable. Similarly, if your aim in life is God-realization, that is your ticket, goal and destination. While you are embarking on this journey, make yourself comfortable. To make yourself comfortable on the spiritual journey, deal with the duality, tension, anxieties and worries of the mind. Ensure that they do not have a negative effect on your body and mind so you can retain optimum health.

This is where sadhana and the goal given by the guru come together. Sadhana helps to manage the ills of the mind, and the goal to focus on is the transcendental, divine attainment, that 'I wish to become that, I wish to realize that'. The goal and the aspiration can be the awakening of spiritual awareness; however, you have to manage the fine details and events that affect and shape your life on a daily basis. Maintaining the balance between what you are doing today and the goal that you are aspiring for is the real sadhana. Do not disconnect the goal from the sadhana of today, thinking 'This is not going to take me there.'

The goal given by the guru or by oneself has to be in accordance with the aspirations to attain greater heights, purity, balance and harmony in life. This was the guideline given by Swami Sivananda when he identified the traits of mind. His book, *Mind: Its Mysteries and Control* is like the Bible for those who wish understand the mind and its traits and behaviours. He has defined and outlined methods for dealing with each and every tamasic expression and experience of the mind.

A spiritual lifestyle

Swami Sivananda was a medical doctor. In that capacity he cured many people, but this did not satisfy him, as he realized that he was healing only the body. The lack in people's lives, due to which they suffered from physical and mental diseases, could not be cured through medical science. He found the way when he understood that matter cannot be cured by matter, but by spirituality. Shortly afterwards, he left his position as a doctor.

To heal matter through the spirit is a beautiful idea and concept. When Swami Sivananda took sannyasa and established the ashram, he inspired a collection of disciples and followers gathered around him with three principles. The first was to serve; the second was to love everyone; and the third was to give, believing that others' suffering was one's own. These are the three cardinal teachings of Swami Sivananda. This sadhana involves the fine-tuning of the dualistic mind so that it becomes capable of experiencing the higher qualities. These higher qualities represent spiritual life, which for Swami Sivananda begins first with service, then love, then giving, and thereafter purity arises.

Serve: Humans work all their life, the aim of which is to fulfil self-oriented needs. When work is not based on selfish needs but connected to the feeling of selflessness, it becomes service. When you eat food for yourself, it is a selfish act. When you give food to others, it becomes a selfless act. When you heal yourself, it is a selfish act; when you heal others, it is an act of service.

Service is seva; however, service is also action. It is the change of perception in the action that converts it into *seva*, selfless service. When the perceptions are self-oriented, then that selfish vritti makes you go through action and reaction.

Swami Sivananda says that in order to bring balance in the normal actions of life, perform them as seva. This will create a new way of thinking, behaviour and conduct. Once you take the first step, the next will follow in a natural way.

In the beginning, if an individual's actions are disconnected just a little from selfishness and connected a little to selflessness, it's enough. In work that is one hundred percent selfish, try to make it ten or twenty percent selfless. What will happen with eighty percent selfishness and twenty percent selflessness? Even that small percentage will help you come out of the selfish vritti, and your actions will take on the form of seva. Your actions will no longer be for satisfying yourself, or for your selfish purposes; they will be for others. When work becomes service, it brings happiness and joy into the lives of others, and they bless you for it.

Action geared towards oneself is known as karma and action geared towards others, with the attitude of selflessness, is known as seva. The action is the same; the attitude and perception changes. Swami Sivananda says that as you excel more in this expression, gradually keep reducing the percentage of selfishness and increase selflessness. Eventually, all your actions will become seva, not only for others, but also for yourself. The form and the quality of your actions will change. Make the effort to stop thinking about yourself and think of others for five minutes in a twenty-four hour day.

Love: The real and only connection in this world is the connection of love. With whomever you have that connection, you feel them as your own. With the connection of love you begin to see yourself in the other person. If there is no love then distance is created; when there is love, distances are bridged. The strength of a true human being is the love that unites, and not love which separates and creates different identities.

You love those who are close to you. It is difficult to love those whom you do not consider your own. You can be friends with them, still you will not be able to love them the way you love your own family. Sri Swamiji says that only one who understands the suffering of others, who empathizes with others and tries to free others from their suffering, can grow, expand and evolve. Only that person can experience the Supreme, Universal Spirit within.

When one experiences God, it is natural to experience love, as ultimately every individual loves God alone. You may see your God in any form, but at the end you see God in the whole creation. This experience connects you with every being, and the whole world becomes your family. Love removes duality and creates unity. It makes you compassionate towards others and understand their suffering, so you try to help them according to your capacity. After all, the squirrel had also contributed to the building of the bridge in the story of the *Ramayana*. The great warriors Nala, Neela, Angad and Hanuman were bringing huge mountains and rocks, and the small squirrel was bringing in grains of sand to fill in the gaps. A person must contribute according to their own capacity.

Give: As you become more selfless and more loving, you become more giving, and what you give helps other people find and discover happiness in their life. What will you give? You will give that which will lessen the lack and bring auspiciousness in others' lives. The sigh of a sufferer can become a curse for you and his smile your biggest boon. The choice is yours, whether you want to receive the curse or the boon. The curse will separate you; the boon will unite you. The absence of love will create separation, whereas the presence of love will create unity.

With serving, loving and giving, you become selfless. As you become selfless, you become pure. As you become pure, you become good. As you become good, you do good. As you do good, you begin to understand, realize and accept the beauty of this world and the divine, the *saundarya* aspect of God. That eventually merges you with God. Thus, the eight stages of Swami Sivananda's eightfold path of yoga are: serve, love, give, purify, do good, be good, meditate, realize. The same method has been given in the scriptures; however,

Swami Sivananda has made the teachings of the scriptures relevant and applicable to the present times. This is the beginning of spirituality in an individual's life.

Role of women

Just as the body needs two legs to walk and move around, you need two legs to walk forward in spiritual life. One leg is named *bhakti* or devotion and the second is *shakti* or strength. What kind of devotion? Like that of Hanuman. What kind of strength? Like that of Angad. Nobody could move Angad once he put his foot on a particular spot. The biggest warriors in Ravana's army lost against him.

Whether one is a householder or a sannyasin, both need devotion and strength. Devotion enhances the emotional sensitivity and gives a direction to the emotions, while strength provides the capacity to live life properly. What is the source of devotion and strength? Sri Swamiji says women are the source and centre of devotion and strength. He always said that it is necessary to uplift women; otherwise, society cannot be built. Men do not build society as by nature they are cruel and aggressive. They will use a stick first and think later.

Women are not cruel; they are soft. They have compassion and sensitivity. All your life you look for the quality of softness. When you want something or have a problem, you go to your mother and tell her about it. A mother is the image of sensitivity and softness. She expresses love, kindness, affection, compassion and atmabhava naturally.

If this light within women is given the chance to become effulgent, they will use it to uplift their families and build society. They can give good, positive thoughts and samskaras to others and inspire them to do good work. That is why everyone must respect women. Women are the ambassadors of culture, not men. When your daughter gets married and goes to another house, she becomes the ambassador of the culture and samskaras of her house. That is why Sri Swamiji says that you must always remember the contribution of women to society.

It has been written in some books that sannyasins must keep ten arm lengths away from women. To this, Sri Swamiji responded, "Will you stay ten arm lengths away from your mother as well?" No. "Then why don't you look at women in the form of mothers? If you look at women with desire, you will have to stay twenty arm lengths away from them, not just ten. However, if you look at them as mothers, then you can even go and sit on their lap. A mother accepts that." Sri Swamiji had that kind of feeling for women. He used to say that if spirituality becomes one with a mother's sensitivity, and the whole family becomes suffused with beauty, love, positive and virtuous feelings, actions and thoughts, then society will certainly change. It will become a cultured, virtuous and spiritual society.

Awakening of Spiritual Awareness

Morning, 8 March 2013

This year completes fifty years since the establishment of the Bihar School of Yoga. The purpose of the journey that the Bihar School of Yoga has completed in the last fifty years has been the dissemination of spirituality. Fifty years ago in Munger, while laying the foundation of the yoga ashram, Sri Swamiji said that this ashram had a spiritual mission. He did not say that this was a religious institution. He said, "We are laying the foundations of a spiritual mission, for which we need help from all of you. The spread of spirituality is the aim, purpose and goal of this yoga ashram." Saying this, he clarified that attaining spiritual awareness is the goal of human life. Today, seeing the work that is being done through the yoga ashram, it can be said that a spiritual revolution is being created in the lives of people all over the world.

Teachings of *Bhagavad Gita*

In the *Bhagavad Gita,* Sri Krishna explained to Arjuna on the battlefield the meaning of karma, duty, devotion and knowledge. Some call the *Bhagavad Gita* a religious book; some call it a philosophical treatise. Irrespective, reading it is likely to improve your actions in life. Arjuna was confused, but after receiving the wisdom contained in this discourse, he was able to develop balance and perform his karma.

Life is determined by karma. The scriptures say that life and the circumstances of life are the result of karma. If you

are happy today, it is the result of past karma. If there is disturbance, anguish and suffering, then that too is a result of your past karma. You create karma from birth to death, and karma is never finished. In fact, karma gets you more entangled in the world. Why does this happen?

Sri Krishna says that because your karma is not offered to the higher reality that you are entangled in karma. Sri Krishna has even connected karma to God. Arjuna asks, "Why are we drawn towards the world of the senses and sense objects?" Krishna replies, "It is because you have never disciplined your emotions. First, learn to manage your emotions." Arjuna says that while being infatuated with maya, a person forgets his duty. Why does this happen? Krishna replies, "You feel that the material world of the senses is everything, so there is infatuation with it. If you make God the basis of your life, you will be free from the negative effects of infatuation or attachment."

In this manner, whatever practical question Arjuna asks, Krishna gives the same answer: cultivate the feeling that every act you perform in life is a yajna. What is the outcome of a yajna? It brings auspiciousness and goodness in everyone's life. Your actions must be auspicious and good for everyone. In saying this, Sri Krishna is trying to draw attention to the sattwic potential hidden within you.

When your sattwic light is kindled, when you become soft and sensitive, then you will understand what Sri Krishna is saying and live according to it. When God gives instructions, the purpose is to enable you to attain fullness or completeness in life. Sri Krishna's message is: do everything, but with a feeling of non-attachment and duty, yet with faith and full participation. Believe that what you are doing is a yajna that will bring wellbeing and auspiciousness to everyone and establish dharma.

This kind of awareness of your karma and conduct is spirituality, the flowering of which connects you with a higher, universal power instead of the world of senses and sense objects. Once you become God-oriented, your life becomes surrendered to that divine, transcendental force. This is the message of the *Bhagavad Gita*.

Difference between a sadhu and a householder

Spirituality is a process. It is a process of realizing the self by attaining purity and by modifying one's mental expressions, attitudes and behaviours to attain inner peace. It is a process of managing the vrittis of the mind. This is the foundation for everyone, whether sannyasins or householders.

Every person, whether a sannyasin or a householder, must face external circumstances in life and struggle to move forward. Both start with the same mindset, samskaras, impressions and aspirations. How they differ is in the desire for a reward or the lack of it, the feeling of selfishness and selflessness. A householder acquires and collects objects while an ascetic gives away possessions. A householder likes to accumulate things to feel prosperous, even though it may be an illusion. A sadhu has given up collecting and has a giving nature. If the renunciate accumulates, it is only for the purpose of giving.

The circumstances are the same, only the mentality and perspectives are different. The householder's mentality is influenced and controlled by *bhoga*, enjoyment; the renunciate's mentality is led by *yoga*, union. When enjoyment is the dominant state in a householder, that individual is known as a worldly person, a *bhogi*. When the pull of yoga is powerful in a householder, then he is considered a good, virtuous person. The renunciate in whom enjoyment is a strong condition is called a fraud, and the renunciate who is absorbed in yoga is a saint.

One state connects and engrosses the individual in the world whereas the other bestows liberation. The state of bhoga binds and entangles you with the world so you are only thinking of 'me and mine'. The state of yoga heralds spirituality in your life so you recognize the existence of God in your life as *sat-chit-ananda*, truth-consciousness-bliss. The purpose of spirituality is to invoke peace and strength in life, and create a strong connection with the *ishta*, the chosen form of divinity.

The attributes of peace, strength and connection are as important for a householder as for a sadhu. Every person wishes for peace, happiness, comfort and conveniences. Every person wants the capacity, strength and ability to fulfil all responsibilities and be recognized in society. Every person wants to establish a relationship through which he will be recognized. The sadhu, however, associates all these aspects with the divine rather than the world. He forms a relationship with God, receives strength from God, and the experience of peace takes him closer to God.

If everyone is aspiring to cultivate spiritual awareness, what is the way to go about it? Every person has to cross the bridge between material life and spiritual life. This is the process of sadhana. The number of steps you need to take to reach from one end of the bridge to the other will depend on how you walk. Nevertheless, when you start walking the path away from the world towards the realm of the spirit, first you need to take the help of yoga.

Purpose of yoga sadhana

The answer to discovering spirituality is found in a broad vision of yoga, not merely in the practice of yoga. Yoga approaches three dimensions of human personality: the physical, the psychological, and the spiritual; body, mind, and spirit. Yoga constitutes a complete system to fulfil the needs of human nature, provided you can apply it in the right manner. If this is done, the benefits and the outcome of yoga are spontaneous and natural.

To create a garden of flowers, the ground must be prepared and the seeds planted. When the flowers bloom, the colour, beauty and fragrance will be a natural outcome. You do not have to work to bring out the colour or fragrance of flowers; that is the natural result of growth. The effort required is in planting the seed, looking after it and protecting it. In the same manner, the integral yoga conceived by Swami Sivananda, and taken further by Swami Satyananda, helps to manage the physical conditions which become a barrier in the creative expression of the senses. Through a combination of practices, you are able to experience physical health, mental peace, and bliss of the soul. This is the beginning of spiritual awareness.

Many people come to yoga, but not everybody comes with spiritual aspirations. Most people come to practise yoga sadhana with a specific purpose: to be free of illness, tension or mental stress, and they are not thinking about the path of spirituality. They only wish to eradicate their problem, to find relief from their problems. Yet, in the fifteen-day, one-month, or four-month training in yoga, learning asana, pranayama, relaxation and concentration, their health improves. Something happens within them, and they become aware of a different aspect of themselves, of the world and the reality that they live in. Although they are learning asana, pranayama, pratyahara and dharana, they discover something that makes them interested in spiritual life.

What they discover is that if they follow the yogic system implicitly and explicitly, they gain physical wellbeing. Sri

Swamiji used to say that nothing is impossible for yoga, provided you follow the rules to the letter. Even management of illness is possible with one hundred percent efficacy. The only condition is that the rules must be followed as given by yoga, which most practitioners do not do. When you follow the rules of yoga, it no longer remains only a physical practice; it becomes a psychological and spiritual effort as well. With practice of a combination of asana, pranayama, mudra, bandha, pratyahara, dharana, relaxation, concentration, mantra and other practices, it is possible to access the physical body, the psychological dimension and the spiritual dimension. The experience of yoga in the physical body is that of health and wellbeing. The experience of yoga in the mind is that of peace and contentment. Through the yogic techniques of relaxation and concentration, the mind is freed from worry, tension, pain, indiscipline and dissipation that cause illness, and it becomes healthy once again. As the mental dissipations cease and the body gains health, the mental energy increases.

The yogic texts say that there is *prana shakti*, vital force, in the body and *chitta shakti*, force of consciousness, in the mind. The strength of prana is gross and that of chitta is subtle. Just as electricity can run a large machine as well as a sensitive computer, the energy within you regulates the body in the form of prana shakti and the mind in the form of chitta shakti. The practice of yoga creates a balance between the two, driving out physical sickness and mental tension. The mind becomes peaceful, the body becomes healthy, and bliss, happiness, contentment and wholeness are experienced. You become more aware of every condition of your life, and you are able to consciously work for your wellbeing and peace.

The experience of yoga in the physical body is that of health and wellbeing, in the mind is that of peace and contentment, and in the dimension of spirit is that of a creative nature and resilience of wisdom in various conditions and situations of life. Through the awakening of spiritual awareness, a pure, positive, creative and constructive state emerges. When resilience of wisdom is attained, the harshness and hardness of the intellect softens and a greater awareness and understanding develops. This allows you to manage your life better. As a result, a music composer is able to create more beautiful music, a mathematician develops a sharper intellect, a worker becomes more efficient, and a sadhu becomes an even better sadhu. There is excellence in behaviour and work. This is the result of inner peace and freedom from tension.

Thus, yoga has an important role to play in the cultivation of spiritual awareness, although that may not be the initial intention when you take up yoga. Even if you leave yoga, the experience that you had of the mind and beyond the mind will be a memory that will bring you back to realize and regain that experience, even after ten or twenty years. This leads to personal change and transformation. When the mind has attained a bit of peace, then its creative nature makes the effort to create new samskaras in life, which aid in your evolution and spiritual growth.

Laying the spiritual foundation in children

Sri Swamiji says that if you want to improve your home and look after your family, society, nation and the world at large, your children must be given good samskaras. Adults have become rigid, their nature and personalities are conditioned and set. Even if you use a hammer and chisel, it will not be possible to transform them, as the shape has already been formed. If the hammer and chisel are used forcibly, the form will break. In small children, the shape is yet to be formed, and it can be given a positive direction through samskaras. If the right samskaras are given to children, in a couple of generations a beautiful culture and environment can be created in society.

Sri Swamiji always paid attention to the upbringing of children, whether in Munger or in Rikhia. In Munger, the children of Bal Yoga Mitra Mandal learn yoga and receive many other positive inputs at the ashram, and they fulfil

all their duties faithfully. Through all the activities they participate in, they receive samskaras. These samskaras will help build a beautiful and creative mentality within them later. They will never lack confidence or talent, and in the future will certainly contribute as outstanding citizens.

Therefore, pay attention to the samskaras you give to children. In the Indian tradition, samskaras are imparted through initiating children in the practices of surya namaskara, nadi shodhana pranayama and Gayatri mantra. If done properly, just these three practices will enable them to connect with their inner nature and tap the source of creativity. You must give children the opportunity to naturally express the divinity within. In the ashram they receive this opportunity, and you can see that they all sparkle like bright flowers.

Planting the seeds of spirituality in the family

Mothers: It is one duty to give samskaras to children, and another is the creation of discipline in the house by the mothers. These are the commands of Sri Swamiji for inculcating positive samskaras in children. Mothers have to play an important role as they are the ambassadors of culture. Mothers have the biggest responsibility to improve society, bring about wellbeing in the family, and preserve culture. The guru can only present a thought and an inspiration, it is the mother who has to give new samskaras at home, and for this, there has to be order in the house.

To create a spiritual ambience and environment at home, it is necessary for mothers to connect the family at least once a week, whether on a Saturday, Monday, or a holiday, and together chant a mantra, say the Mahamrityunjaya mantra, one mala, without fail. Invite all the members of your family and take a solemn resolve for happiness, peace and health, chant:

Om tryambakam yajaamahe sugandhim pushtivardhanam
Urvaarukamiva bandhanaat mrityormuksheeya maamaritaat.

This will create a spiritual, inner bonding, and the sankalpa for health, peace and prosperity will come alive. The sankalpa of the mother is the most powerful in a home. The sankalpa of the father may not fructify, but the sankalpa taken by the mother for the family is never ignored by the higher power, as she is the storehouse of love and sensitivity. At home, the mother has this extra duty to ensure that the family members imbibe a spiritual culture, and that can only happen when she becomes the centre of spiritual activities and does not limit herself to cooking and cleaning.

Once a month, on the full moon day, chant the 'Sundarkand' from *Ramacharitamanas*. The *Ramacharitamanas* is not just a mythological story of someone born thousands of years ago; it is an incredibly special book. In the verses of the *Ramacharitamanas* are hidden sabar mantras. These are mantras of immense power that give instant benefit and result. Only knowledgeable people are aware of the sabar mantras within the text. Nevertheless, when the *Ramacharitamanas* is chanted, the effect of those sabar mantras changes lives instantly, even for those who do not know them.

When Sri Swamiji was in isolation in Rikhia, doing the sadhana of panchagni, one day he said, "I have read many books, imbibed a lot of knowledge, and learnt a lot about man, God and religion, but my mind never felt satisfied. I always felt something was lacking. However, when I started the chanting of *Ramacharitamanas* in the correct form, I realized that I did not need to read or know anything more. The full meaning of life and God is given in this easy and incomparable book."

When Sri Swamiji said this, I did not understand what he meant. I have also chanted the *Ramacharitamanas* many times, and done akhanda paths. Still, I was not able to understand his deep words. This year when I was doing the panchagni, I chanted the *Ramacharitamanas* during the sadhana and completed three rounds of nine-day readings of the full text. During the first reading, I was absorbed in the story. In the second reading, I observed that my mental state had changed. In the first reading, the words appeared as they do: black inscriptions on white paper, but in the second reading they did not appear in that form. Instead, it seemed as if the words, couplets, stanzas and slokas were written in jewel-encrusted letters, and were sparkling. It was as if each page was a storehouse of precious stones. When I read it the third time, my awareness became even more subtle.

I am telling you about this experience with the *Ramacharitamanas* as I see myself as a seeker and a laboratory, and have made an effort to understand how change comes about in one's awareness and life through a process of sadhana. When the third reading was taking place, my awareness had become so subtle that I started to see the sabar mantras. If this process had continued, it is possible that I would have glimpsed, experienced and learnt many more things.

Whatever Sri Rama may have been: a child, a king, an avatara, or a *maryada purushottam*, an ideal man, the *Ramacharitamanas* is an unparalleled book. It depicts Rama's character as the culmination of spiritual thinking and understanding. The methods of spirituality are contained in a hidden manner in the form of the mantras. As one connects with the chanting, the effects of the mantras start playing on the awareness, and they awaken new areas of consciousness, leading one towards enlightenment and liberation.

Never take the *Ramacharitamanas* lightly as just a storybook or a historic text. Its incidents may be historic, but the benefit that you receive from chanting it, the satisfaction, happiness and peace that you gain from it, will never be had from any other literature, scripture or philosophy anywhere in the world.

Over centuries, it has been the experience of people in society that the chanting of 'Sundarkand', one of the chapters of the *Ramacharitramanas,* brings peace and joy, and fulfils all desires. Whether or not you understand what you chant, whether you believe in Rama or not, it does not matter. The chanting will give you the result. Therefore, every Poornima, chant the *Ramacharitramanas*.

The first program for the family is the chanting of the Mahamrityunjaya mantra, once a week. The second is the chanting of the 'Sundarkand', once a month on the full moon day. There is a third routine that can be included in

the timetable. For one day, mothers must go on strike at home and everyone must fast. This is beneficial for physical health. If you flush the toilet four times a day, water will flow out four times. If you flush it fifty times a day, water will flow out fifty times. The less you use it, the longer it will last and will remain useful to you. The more it is used, the greater the chances of malfunction.

The stomach works on the same principle. Usually, you are always munching something or the other. The more the mouth works, the more upset the stomach will be. Whether you eat a full plate of food or one grain of rice, the digestive juices flow in the same quantity. A person whose mouth is constantly working will tend to suffer from acidity, gas or some other form of indigestion. A human being is more likely to die due to a full stomach than an empty one!

For this reason, if you do not cook food for one day a week and make do with a fruit diet, it will be good for health. After a couple of months it will become a habit and no one will even complain about being hungry. If you think it is difficult to do this every week, it is enough to do it once a month or on Ekadashi. In this way, the tongue, taste, temptation and greed can be regulated.

Children: As previously mentioned, children should practise three things every day: surya namaskara, nadi shodhana pranayama and the Gayatri mantra. These three practices should form a discipline in the lives of children. In the same way that one gets up in the morning, takes a bath and has breakfast, surya namaskara should be practised each morning. This will help regulate the physical energy of children. Along with this, they should do at least five rounds of nadi shodhana pranayama, which will improve their intelligence, memory and brain. With the chanting of the Gayatri mantra, they will acquire wisdom and positive qualities.

Fathers and men: Men often suffer from high blood pressure. That is because their head is always hot, they are easily irritated, angered and inflamed. To manage their hypertension caused by worry and anxiety, they can reflect on the events of day at night before going to sleep, count the breaths, and empty the mind. If the mind is emptied at night before sleep, then its inherent creative powers will manifest. If there is a lid on the mind at the time of sleep, then the subtle powers of mind will not manifest.

To help remove the mental tension, follow this method. When you go to bed, lie on your back in shavasana. For two minutes visualize the whole body, then loosen and relax it. Now, recall all the incidents that took place during the day: 'In the morning, I woke up at such time, did this, wore those clothes, had this for breakfast, said these things, left the house at that time, met these people, went with so and so person.' On the screen of the mind, see all the incidents that took place from morning to evening: what kind of conversations you had, with whom you behaved lovingly, with whom you fought, what you liked and what you disliked. After seeing the whole day's incidents and situations, when you come to the point of 'I am now lying on my bed and doing this practice', observe your breath and watch the navel rising and falling with the breath. Count the breath backwards from fifty to one and then go to sleep.

This seemingly easy and simple method is a powerful practice through which tensions in body and mind are removed. By creating the relaxation, you are able to sleep peacefully. The predominant cause of high blood pressure is worry, anxiety, stress and pressure. If you can remove or minimize these, the mind will become calm and quiet. Try this for a week. If you do not like it, leave it; if there is an improvement, continue with it.

The mind is energy and when it is free of tension at night, it heals the body as you rest. If the mind is under tension, worry and anxiety, then the healing capacity of the mind diminishes. If you want the mind to possess healing powers, remember to empty the mind of tensions every night before sleep. With the attainment of peace in this manner, gradually you will become aware of another reality, of another experience that makes you feel better, happier and content.

That will be the spiritual reality. Yoga is the beginning of the journey into the awakening of spiritual awareness.

These three programs are for eradicating tension, establishing a beautiful environment at home, and facilitating the flowering of talents in children. Through the medium of yoga, the ashram has been doing this work for the last fifty years to bestow health and peace, instil positive, sattwic qualities in people, help them discover the light within, and promote a disciplined and awakened spiritual life in the material world. Slowly, as the mind is drawn deeper into spirituality, the sadhana also changes, the thinking changes, the routines change, the environment changes. Someone becomes a sannyasin, someone becomes a good householder. However, the truth of life, the foundation of life is to develop positive samskaras and culture. Spirituality grows only through samskaras and culture.

Secret of God-Realization

Afternoon, 8 March 2013

This year, the Golden Jubilee of the Bihar School of Yoga is being celebrated in Munger. The role and contribution of the Bihar School of Yoga has been to disseminate the knowledge of yoga to awaken the spiritual awareness in people. However, the foundation of yoga and spirituality was laid in Munger much before the ashram was created. Sri Swamiji undoubtedly gave a concrete form to the sankalpa of the Bihar School of Yoga, yet its foundation was laid in 1937.

On 25th January 1937, our paramguru Swami Sivananda came to Munger and stayed here for a week. Between 25th and 30th January, he conducted programs of sankirtan and satsangs in various places, especially on the town hall grounds. If you go through his old books, where there is a mention of his satsang and sankirtan in Munger, you will find one sentence on sadhana and devotion that he told the public of Munger. This same sentence took a concrete form twenty-five years later when Sri Swamiji established the ashram in 1963.

Swami Sivananda had said, "The aim of life is devotion to God. You attain peace through devotion to God. In order to nurture the seed of peace in your life, you have to protect it from wild animals. These wild animals take the form of greed, lust, obstinacy, whimsicality, irritability, and so on, and make your mind restless. That is why you need to look after your mind, protect it, make yourself pure, reflect, meditate, and finally experience oneness with God."

When Swami Sivananda's footsteps fell in Munger, the foundation of his teachings was laid here. Upon this foundation, Sri Swamiji established the ashram in 1963. At that time he said that when yoga was a part of the lives of the people of India, there was wellbeing, prosperity and peace in Indian society. When people stopped practising yoga, dissatisfaction, suffering and poverty came in. Therefore, the Bihar School of Yoga aims to spread the knowledge of yoga to contribute in uplifting the nation's culture.

Aim of yoga

Inspired by this feeling, Sri Swamiji established the Bihar School of Yoga. People would ask him, "What will we gain from the asana, pranayama and meditation that you teach?" He would reply that through the practices the potential and capacity of the human mind will increase and it will be purified.

In 1965, an International Yoga Convention was conducted here. The Shankaracharya of Puri had come and he asked Sri Swamiji a question, "You teach yoga practices and karma yoga to your disciples. Is it possible to attain liberation through yoga practices and karma yoga?" Sri Swamiji replied, "Revered One, you are the acharya of our tradition, you are superior to me; however, my opinion and belief is that when peace comes into a person's life through the practice of yoga, it will lead the person to embrace divine life and God." If the mind is restless and dissipated, you will never become God-intoxicated. You will only try to remove the mental troubles. God may be used as a support, but experiencing God is not the focus. You may pray to God to provide relief from the suffering; however, you will not be able to contemplate God or practise devotion to God. Once the mind becomes peaceful, it will spontaneously discover devotion and become suffused in it.

As for karma yoga, it is actually *seva*, selfless service. When a person performs actions in the spirit of karma yoga, there is no need to be afraid of the mind. Normally, one is constantly worried about success and failure in every undertaking. When an action is performed without any expectation, only as duty, with faith, love and reverence, there is no need to try to manage the mind. If the mind runs here and there, let it, only maintain the feeling of selflessness and giving. As long as this feeling is present within you, your mind will be inspired to create something good, positive and sattwic. This will bring happiness, peace and satisfaction.

That is why Sri Swamiji says that doing seva makes you feel good. The mind becomes light and free when you perform a selfless action. If you serve someone sincerely, you feel good and happy. You feel happy that for a few moments you have come out of your selfishness and brought happiness into someone else's life. This happiness calms and pacifies all the vrittis and patterns of the mind. This is the purpose of karma yoga.

The answer that Sri Swamiji gave to the Shankaracharya of Puri, contains the essence of his thinking, and has been carried forward by the yoga ashram here. In the last fifty years, the widespread reach of yoga has clearly demonstrated its effectiveness and necessity. People from all over the world come to the Bihar School of Yoga to learn yoga. Even though the main mission of the ashram is yoga, the underlying work is to spread a spiritual culture and impart positive and sattwic samskaras in the lives of people so they may lead a divine life. This has been the real work; yoga has only been a medium.

Three definitions of yoga

The exploration and development of human potential begins with the understanding of the right definitions of yoga and the application of the yogic practices to fulfil those definitions. There are three definitions of yoga.

Efficiency in action: The aim of yoga is not liberation; it is to gain excellence. Thus, the first definition of yoga is: *Yogah karmasu kaushalam* – "Efficiency in action is yoga." Yoga is not just a sadhana; it is also a state of awakening. In the material sense, yoga is being skilful in your work; creativity is the positive expression of work. This definition of yoga corresponds to day-to-day life, family life, social life and professional life. These three aspects surround you from the time of your birth to the time of your death. You are engaged in actions continuously, therefore try to be efficient and discover excellence in your actions. Yoga is efficiency, excellence and creativity in action so you can be satisfied with what you do. This definition of yoga in relation to the normal day-to-day activities of life, is the external expression of yoga, through which you can build your life, family and society. Whether it is health, peace, or freedom from tension, it becomes possible only through skilful work.

Mental equilibrium: The second definition of yoga is: *Samatvam yoga uchyate* – "Maintaining inner equilibrium is the highest form of yoga." Quieten the chatter of your mind and become even-minded. True equanimity is found in the state of non-duality. If you can overcome duality, you will not be disturbed by the suffering and joy in life. Equipoise is a state where the mind is still, concentrated and pure. This involves developing immunity to the negative influences of the environment and the world. Become immune to the influence of success and failure. Maintain your inner equipoise. Maintain your inner clarity. Maintain the resilience of your wisdom, and do not allow it to be trampled by the tension and stresses of life. That is the samatvam aspect, which deals with the psychological behaviour, the management of mental distractions, dissipations, tensions, anxieties, worries, weaknesses and desires. Thus, external efficiency and internal equilibrium are the first two definitions of yoga.

Cultivation of the brahmi vritti: The third definition of yoga is cultivation of the brahmi vritti. People think of yoga as stopping the functions of the mind. This is incorrect. The mind is guided by *vrittis*, the modifications and patterns of the mind; it is never empty. There are always some thoughts, reflections and feelings arising in the mind that bind you to the world, to objects, tensions, worries, troubles, expectations, desires and pleasures. Vrittis are conditions or

states of mind, according to the situation and environment. At night the vritti is *nidra*, sleep. In tension and confusion, the vritti is *viparyaya*, wrong knowledge. In rationality, the vritti is *pramana*, right knowledge. In this manner, each state, behaviour and mood of the mind represents a vritti. The mind can never be devoid of vrittis. The moment the vrittis cease to exist, the experience of the mind will also cease to be. Yoga never speaks of stopping the vrittis. It says, re-channel the vrittis; manage the mental modifications, you do not need to stop the mental modifications. Convert the gross nature into a spiritual nature, the gross vritti into a spiritual vritti. This is known as the *brahmi vritti*, or the cultivation of spiritual awareness.

If a peaceful state arises in the mind, it is the brahmi vritti, for the mind can expand only in a peaceful state. The meaning of *brahma* is an expanding, evolving, blossoming awareness. The word 'brahma' is often connected with God; however, it is derived from the root *brinh,* which means 'constantly expanding awareness'. Brahma or God is that which is constantly evolving and expanding. Identify with the brahmi vritti to liberate the mind from the chains of the negative, tamasic patterns and establish it in sattwa.

These are the three main definitions of yoga, as given by Sri Krishna in the *Bhagavad Gita*, and echoed by other scriptures and sages. The practice of yoga becomes the medium by which you can overcome the conflicts and the dualistic nature of the mind. The tamasic nature is the nature being expressed by you right now; it is the material, gross nature. Through the practice of yoga, you can cultivate the sattwic nature, which is the spiritual nature.

Therefore, the third aspect of yoga, cultivation of the brahmi vritti, is creating a connection with the higher power or God and establishing yourself in sattwa. Once you are established in sattwa, spiritual awareness dawns in your life, and that is the purpose of yoga. In this process, there are many variables that must be dealt with on the way. The little demons that raise their heads from time to time have to be managed properly. These are the demons that poke their head up from the ground, smile at you and tell you, "I am still here. You haven't gotten rid of me."

It is the management of these obstacles to spiritual awareness that eventually sensitizes the human nature and connects one to other beings. it is the state of unity – external, social, emotional, spiritual, which leads to the understanding of the omnipresent nature of the Cosmic Power. With the understanding of the omniscient nature, there is appreciation, respect and recognition of the power of the Supreme Spirit within.

Method to realize God

In the *Bhagavad Gita*, Sri Krishna repeatedly tells Arjuna to surrender himself. Arjuna says, "You keep telling me to surrender. How can I do this, what do I offer?" Krishna says, "Surrender your mind to me." Arjuna says, "That is very difficult. I have not been able to quieten the mind up to this day. My mind always thinks about Duryodhana and

Duhshasana, and about my troubles. Now, as I stand on the battlefield, it is thinking of all that. It is impossible for me to still my mind. Is there any other remedy?"

Krishna says, "If you cannot still the mind, then at least you can think with your intellect that 'I am offering everything to God.' Give your intellect to me. If you cannot offer with your feelings, at least you can pretend to offer with your intellect. This will help you realize that I exist. Once you know that I exist, your intellect will be attracted to me time and again."

Arjuna says, "If my intellect was in the right place, why would I ask you this question to begin with? You are saying that I should give my intellect to you, but my intellect is in turmoil. If my intellect was balanced, I would not sink into depression; I would not forget my duty. How can I possibly connect this confused intellect? Show me another way."

Krishna says, "Fine, do not connect your mind, do not connect your intellect, just be with Me." What is the meaning of 'be with me'? Faith, such strong faith that you can be with the Supreme Spirit all the time, without using the mind or the intellect.

Power of faith

Once upon a time, there lived a poor mother in a village. She had an eight-year-old son. The boy was admitted to a school that was ten kilometres away from home. To get to school, he had to walk through a path that crossed a forest, a mountain and a river. He would walk by himself each day to reach school and return in the evening. Sometimes, while crossing the forest, he would hear the sound of wild animals and become scared.

One day in a frightened state, he came to his mother and said, "Mother, I won't go to school." The mother asked why. He said, "I feel very scared to walk alone. The path is dangerous and I have no friend to walk me across. I am the only one from this village who goes to the school." The mother said, "Son, why don't you call your brother?" The boy asked, "I have a

brother?" The mother replied, "Yes son, you have a brother." The boy said, "But how come I've never seen my brother?" The mother said, "Your brother has a lot of work. He grazes cows all day long. That is why he doesn't come home. He lives in the forest with the cows. The next time you pass through the forest, call out to your brother. If he hears your voice, he will walk you to school and back every day."

The little boy was very happy to learn that he had a brother. The next day, he left for school running along merrily. When he reached the edge of the forest, he called out loudly, "Brother, where are you? Please come. I am alone and scared." Nothing happened, no one came. The poor boy came home crying and told his mother, "Mother, I couldn't see my brother anywhere. I called out to him many times, but he did not come. What is my brother's name? Is it possible there are many 'brothers' there?" His mother consoled him and told him, "Your brother's name is Gopal."

The next morning, the simple-hearted boy went once again towards the forest and standing there called out, "Brother Gopal, where are you? I'm feeling scared and alone." After calling out a number of times, he started crying, "Brother Gopal, why haven't you come?"

As he was crying, he heard the sound of music at a distance, as if someone was playing a flute. That sound gradually came closer. Finally, he saw a handsome boy about thirteen years old, wearing a yellow cloth over his shoulders, playing the flute and walking towards him. When he reached the young boy, he said, "I am your brother Gopal. Tell me, what do you want?"

The boy said, "I need your help on the journey to school and back. Brother, where were you until now?" Gopal said, "I have a lot of work. I graze the cows; the cows keep running away, so I have to go looking for them. That is why I am not able to meet you. But now I am here. Come, let us go to school together." They both walked to school. When school was over, Gopal again met the boy and walked him back through the forest. This became a daily routine.

The school was planning an annual function, and the principal told all the students to bring milk from their houses for the celebration. "We'll make kheer and share it with everyone," he said. All the children arranged to bring milk from their houses. Some said they would bring one glass full, others said they would bring one mug, and yet others said they would bring a bucketful.

This little boy reached home and said to his mother, "Mother, I need a little milk." The mother said, "Son, there's not a drop of milk in the house, why don't you ask your brother Gopal for some?" The boy said, "Mother, you are right. My brother grazes the cows so he would have a lot of milk, I will go and ask him."

The next day he said to Gopal, "Brother Gopal, the principal has asked us to take some milk to school. We do not have a drop of milk at home; please give me a little milk." Gopal gave him a tiny amount of milk in a small earthen cup and said, "I have distributed all the milk. This is all that is left, you take it."

The boy took the cup to school, offered it to his teacher, and said, "Sir, I have brought milk." The principal looked at the small earthen cup and then at the place where big glasses, mugs and buckets full of milk were kept. He became angry, "What will we do with such little milk?" Saying this he struck out his hand. The cup slipped out of the boy's hand and fell to the floor. As the milk fell on the floor, from that small cup an endless stream of milk began to flow. When the principal saw this, he was stunned. He asked the boy, "Who gave you this milk?" The boy said, "My brother Gopal gave it to me."

The teacher felt the urge to meet the brother to find about this unusual occurrence. He said, "I need to meet your brother. Will you take me to him?" The boy said, "Come with me to the forest. I will call my brother and he will come. You can meet him then. He may even give you some more milk." The boy set out for the forest with his teacher. When they reached the middle of the forest, he stopped and called out, "Brother Gopal, someone has come to meet you." Of course, Gopal would not come. He has a peculiar nature. He thinks, 'If there is someone with you, why do you need me? I come only when you have no one with you.'

There is a similar instance of this. During the assembly of the Kauravas, when Draupadi was calling out to others to help her, Krishna remained quiet. Disappointed with everyone and utterly defeated, she called out to Krishna, and he immediately came to her aid. He has only one principle: 'If you depend on someone else, then I am not needed.'

The teacher and the boy stood in the forest, and the boy kept calling out for Gopal with no result. The teacher was getting impatient. He said, "Where is your brother? Why hasn't he come yet? You are lying." The child felt even more hurt. He started crying aloud, "Brother, no one believes what I am saying. Please come, my teacher is here to meet you." While he was saying this, he heard the sound of music. He saw Gopal emerge from behind a tree, and walk towards them. The little boy was very happy. He said, "My brother is here. Teacher, look!"

The teacher could not see anything. He said, "Where is your brother?" The boy replied, "He's right here in front of us. See how beautiful he is. He wears a turban on his head with a peacock feather to adorn it. There is a yellow drape on his shoulders, he is carrying a flute in his hand, and he has a bewitching smile." The teacher, however, could not see anything. The child started crying, "Brother, why can't my teacher see you?" Gopal said, "Your teacher is not able to see me because he wants to see me with his mind and intellect, not with his heart."

The boy said, "Gopal, even if he is not able to see you with his heart, please give him your darshan just once, so he knows I am not lying." Gopal said, "I will not give darshan, but I will play my flute for him once. When he hears the sound of the flute, he will know that I am here." Saying this, he played his flute. The principal heard that sweet melody and lost consciousness. Who will not go mad hearing that divinely sweet melody?

God has said, "If you call me from your heart, I will always be there by your side." When you wish to call God, do not call him with your mind or intellect, call him from the heart. If you can connect your mind, it will be a good thing; however, only a yogi is able to connect his mind. If you become a yogi, you will be able to do so. If you can connect your intellect, that too will be good, yet only a householder can connect his intellect. The intellect is used for give and take. The householder bargains with God, "You do this work of mine and I will feed you sweets and delicious dishes." The devotee does not have a mind or intellect, only feelings of the heart. One who calls out to God from his heart, one who is devoted to Him, will always find Him by his side. Only such a one is able to see God.

God has indicated these three paths: "Fix your mind on me; if you cannot do this then offer your intellect to me; if that also cannot be done, then open the door of your heart and call out to me." Now, Arjuna did not have the courage to ask Krishna how to open the door of the heart. Nevertheless, Krishna has explained this in his teachings. He says, "Know that the world you are living in is maya, and also know that the soul inside you is My reflection. See My reflection within you. Live in the world but look within." If you can do this, you will realize the Universal Spirit in your life. Spirituality will awaken in your life and you will become a true human being. Yoga will no longer remain a practice; it will become a worship of life. This is real spirituality.